— LEARNING AND WORKING —

LEARNING AND WORKING

The occupational socialization of nurses

Kath M. Melia

Tavistock Publications

First published in 1987 by
Tavistock Publications Ltd
11 New Fetter Lane,
London EC4P 4EE

Printed and Bound in Great
Britain by Biddles Ltd,
Guildford and Kings Lynn

*British Library Cataloguing in
Publication Data*

Melia, Kath M.
Learning and working: the
occupational socialization of
nurses.
1. Nursing—Social aspects
I. Title
305.9'613   RT86.5

ISBN 0-422-60130-6

*To the memory of
my father*

CONTENTS

ACKNOWLEDGEMENTS

This book is based on my PhD thesis. The original research was supported by the Scottish Home and Health Department, as part of the core programme of research in the Nursing Studies Research Unit in the University of Edinburgh. I would like to thank my supervisors Lisbeth Hockey, the then director of the Unit, and Dorothy Baker, University of Manchester, for their efforts on my behalf.

I owe the greatest debt of gratitude to the students I interviewed; they made me very welcome and provided such rich data. To friends and colleagues who have encouraged and occasionally nagged me to complete this work – thank you. Particular thanks go to Robert Dingwall for his comments on various drafts. Lastly, my thanks to Gill Davies for her faith in this book and to Caroline Lane for her encouragement and patient assistance.

INTRODUCTION

One of the abiding problems of occupational socialization has to do with the differences between the idealized version of work as it is presented to new recruits and the work as it is practised daily by members of the occupation. This book is about occupational socialization in nursing. Its chief concern has to do with how newcomers to nursing are made aware not only of the activities involved in nursing, but also of how nursing is practised on a daily basis by qualified nurses. It takes as its starting point the accounts of nursing which students in training gave of their experiences of becoming nurses. The book operates on two levels. It addresses questions which on the face of it appear to be of interest only to a nursing audience, but which have underlying them the more general sociological concerns of occupational socialization. It also considers the processes involved in the organization of nursing work. In other words, the socialization of recruits into nursing is treated as a paradigm case in the sociology of work and occupations. In describing nursing as they saw it, the students revealed it to be a divided occupational group whose organization presents considerable problems for those attempting to gain acceptance into its ranks. This raises questions for the whole occupational group. Although the student voice is relatively weak, it demands attention since it represents both a major element of today's nursing workforce and, perhaps more importantly, tomorrow's qualified nursing service.

A central feature of the students' accounts of nursing is the division which they saw between nursing, as it was presented to them in the college, and nursing as they observed and practised it on the hospital wards. It is clear enough what kind of a difficulty this situation presents for students of nursing. However, if we take a closer look at this division it can be seen to be of interest to nursing in general. By pointing to the division within the occupation, the students have directed attention to a long-standing problem which is inherent in the apprenticeship approach to the training of nurses and staffing of hospital wards.

The structure of nurse training is an historical compromise between the provision of a nursing service and the education of nurses. This compromise makes student nurses both learners and workers. The compromise is rooted in the way in which the nursing service operates in Britain, that is by employing large numbers of students who work under the direction of a much smaller number of qualified staff.

This structure has always been problematic. From time to time enquiries and commissions have been established to consider the complex of problems bound up in the question of nursing recruitment and training and the provision of a hospital nursing service (Lancet 1932, RCN 1943 (Hodder Report), RCN 1964 (Platt Report), DHSS 1972 (Briggs Report), UKCC 1986). These deliberations on nursing have all recognized, some more explicitly than others, that a move towards a greater emphasis upon education than on service provision brings with it problems not only for nursing education, but also for the nursing service. Davies (1978) has argued that the managerial changes which have taken place in nursing, for instance the career structure introduced after the Salmon Report of 1966, represent a maintenance of the status quo when compared with the upheaval that a radical alteration of the organization of nursing education would entail. The division between service and education which the students described is, then, a division within the whole of the occupation of nursing which must be taken seriously by those responsible for policy and planning in health care.

At various times in its development different perspectives on nursing have been canvassed. These approaches to nursing and its teaching have ranged from Florence Nightingale's imperative 'to do the sick no harm' with the demand that nurses be obedient workers, loyal to the matron and hospital, posing no threat to the medical profession, to the present preoccupation with what is known as 'the nursing process'. The latter is an attempt to put nursing practice on a more scientific footing, by taking a problem solving approach to the planning, effecting and evaluation of care. It accompanies moves within nursing to create a knowledge base which is independent of medicine and to promote the notion of autonomous nursing activity. The idea that nurses might be responsible for their practice rather than merely carrying out the orders of the medical staff has caused concern within the medical profession. If nursing is to be recognized within the health care services, it would be advantageous for the group to be able to present a united front to other professionals and to the public. The questions to be asked, then, are 'In whose best interests are these various developments within nursing?' and 'In what direction should, or can, the occupation move?'

It will now have become apparent where the sociologist's interest in this book might lie. Nursing presents not only an occupation into which the recruits must become socialized but also one in which they form a significant part of the workforce. The tension which exists in nursing between curriculum needs and service demands calls for a particular kind of work organization and socialization process. This tension is a daily reality for the students who are faced with competing factions or segments within the occupational group they are preparing to join; each segment presents the student with a different version of nursing work.

Segmentation and the occupation of nursing

The students' account of nursing as it emerges through the analytic categories provides a basis from which to examine the process of socialization into nursing. Much of what the students have to say points to a divided occupational group. This brings us to the main organizing theme of the book – the notion of segmentation in relation to the occupation of nursing.

Bucher and Strauss (1961) argued that it is not entirely useful to assume a relative homogeneity within a profession. There are, they point out, 'many entities, many values and many interests'. They describe professions as 'loose amalgamations of segments pursuing different objectives in different manners'. Developing this theme in a later work Bucher and Stelling (1977:21) define a segment as:

'a sub group within a profession. It is composed of individuals who have in common some professional characteristics and beliefs which distinguish them from members of other segments. Members of a segment share specific professional identity; they also have similar ideas about the nature of their discipline, the relative order of the activities it includes, and its relationship to other fields.'

Hughes (1971: 357) too says that occupations contain such a variety of members with varying perceptions of the work that 'to call them by one name is close to misleading'. We have not got, according to Hughes, 'a fully worked out anatomy of occupational prestige, including all contacts and interactions out of which the images of the various occupations develop'.

Following Bucher and her colleagues, I have used the notion of segmentation as an analytic and organizing device. I shall argue that nursing is an occupation which contains segments similar to those Bucher *et al.* describe in the professions; each with its own particular reason for canvassing the version of nursing which it has made its own. The two main segments are *service* and *education*.

I will sketch some of the main themes of the book so that the reader has some indication of what to look for in what follows. In chapters 2–6 the students' accounts of nursing are discussed in terms of the main analytic categories which emerged from the data. There are five categories which describe how the students 'fitted in' throughout their training. 'Fitting in' emerges as a theme which runs through the analysis as the students described how throughout their training they tried to behave in the way that any given situation demanded. Their concern was to meet the expectations of those in authority and so 'fitting in' constitutes a major part of the students' efforts in negotiating their way through training.

Two main categories describe how the students got along with the ward staff: 'Learning the Rules' has to do with the students learning how to 'pass' as workers to the satisfaction of the permanent staff, whilst 'Getting the Work Done' is primarily concerned with how nursing work is organized and achieved on hospital wards. A third and related category is 'Learning and Working', in which the student's dual role of student of nursing and member of the hospital ward staff is discussed. This category is an attempt to describe the position in which the students find themselves, namely that of *student* doing *nursing* work.

The category 'Just Passing Through' deals with the students' transient position in the nursing service. Students move from ward to ward, from specialty to specialty, unlike the trained and auxiliary staff who tend to work in one area for more lengthy periods of time. Therefore, most of the encounters which students have with the members of the occupational group they are preparing to join are circumscribed by a particular place and time, and are invariably short lived. The transient nature of the students' encounters with permanent staff has implications for the trained staff, for the students themselves, and necessarily for the organizing of nursing work on the wards.

One of the consequences of transiency is that the students felt that they were frequently denied information about patients and so found it difficult to talk to them. Students complained that the patients themselves sometimes knew more about their condition then they did. This aspect of the students' accounts of nursing is described in the category 'Nursing in the Dark'.

Throughout this book I have argued that nursing is too diverse an enterprise to be embraced by one name, and that the occupational group of nurses is too large and heterogeneous a group for its members to share the same view of what their work should be and how it should be organized. It is this segmentation which is responsible for the existence of two different versions of nursing encountered by the students.

As mention has been made of the aspects of this work which are of sociological interest, it might also be said, simply in passing at this juncture, that the issue of professionalization of nursing is addressed in the book. It was never the intention at the outset to deal with the question 'is nursing a profession?'. However, the student nurses described nursing in ways which invited such a line of inquiry and analysis. This work, then, also sheds some light on the student thinking within an occupational group which is making claims to professional status.

Before proceeding to the students' story, it is necessary to give the reader some idea of how this research was undertaken. Those for whom a discussion of research methods holds no fascination need read no further than this short description, which provides sufficient working knowledge of the study to make what follows comprehensible. For readers with an interest in research methodology there is a longer account of the methods employed in this work in the Appendix (pp. 188–96).

The interviews with the student nurses took place over a period of eighteen months and comprise some forty hours of interview tapes. The students interviewed came from two Scottish colleges of nursing and were eight, eighteen, or thirty months into their training for the general register. The students thirty months into their training had already sat their final examinations, but still had six months' experience to gain before registration.

As the matter of registration is raised here, it may be a convenient point to describe, briefly, the mechanics of British nurses' training at the time of this study. The majority of nurses gain their status as qualified registered nurses by following a three year programme of training, which is based in a college of nursing (attached to one or a group of hospitals). A much smaller number take degree courses and achieve registration and a degree either in nursing or in some cognate discipline. The programme is organized in such a way that the students spend periods of six to eight weeks gaining practical experience in various hospital wards and departments, plus a short time with the community health and social services. This practical experience is supported by periods of time spent in the college of nursing, during which they have full-time student existence with lectures, tutorials, and the like. The whole programme is, then, characterized by constant movement as the students go from one clinical area to another and to and from the college of nursing. Whilst the data in this book are drawn from the Scottish system of nurse training, the students' experiences were much the same as those of their contemporaries in other parts of the United Kingdom.

The students became involved in the study on a volunteer basis, and so are not held to be 'representative' or 'typical' in any statistical sense. They were approached during one of their spells in college, the tutors allowing me some time to explain the project to the students and to ask for volunteers to be interviewed. I wanted to create a situation in which the students could tell me freely what they felt about nursing and not merely what they might think a nurse/sociologist would want to hear. Each interview started with a few remarks, which amounted to my saying: 'I'm interested in what student nurses think about nursing', and continued in a conversational style, following an agenda in varying order and picking up the issues that the students raised.

There appear to be at least two ways of handling the kind of data and their interpretation which we are dealing with here. One would be to allow the story to unfold, much as it did as the study progressed, and to save the interpretation and the commentary until the end. This has the appeal of letting the reader absorb the students' story in an uncluttered way. The disadvantage, however, is that the reader would be required to retain a lot of detail before being confronted with any of the interpretive work. An alternative would be to present the data and analysis in discrete bites as we go along, culminating in a grand gathering together in the last chapter. This form of presentation has a 'tidy' kind of appeal, but would in fact be difficult to sustain. It would also be ultimately misleading as it would tend to simplify the interpretation and underplay the linkages to be made between the different sections of the analysis. I have opted, therefore, for something of a middle ground in that I have allowed the students' story to unfold with a fair amount of interpretive comment along the way.

1

LEARNING THE RULES

'On the job training, in and of the every day world, provides a realistic and individualised learning setting. But it does that at the cost of making teaching and learning vulnerable to potent external constraints.'

(Becker 1972: 101)

The students I interviewed described their on-the-job training in some detail. Perhaps the most common and striking feature of the students' accounts of their work experience was their description of the attitude of the permanent staff towards them. The staff made their expectations of students known in a variety of ways, but the plain and simple message seemed to be that students should 'pull their weight' and accomplish a fair share of the ward's work. This chapter is concerned with the students' description of how they learnt to function on the wards, and to play their part as members of the nursing workforce. The category 'learning the rules' serves to explain the data concerned with the on-the-job occupational socialization of the student nurse.

Socialization

Medicine has furnished the sociology of occupations with some of the seminal works on professional socialization. Two classic studies of medical students carried out in Columbia (Merton *et al.* 1957) and Kansas (Becker *et al.* 1961) took different approaches to the business of occupational socialization. Merton and his colleagues focused attention upon the medical school as the socializing agency, and viewed the students as passive recipients of the teaching and experiences offered to them. This view of occupational socialization is perhaps best summed up by Olesen and Whittaker (1968: 5):

'Once the educational system has formally started work on the student, his empty head is filled with values, behaviors, and viewpoints of the profession, the knowledge being perfect and complete by the time of graduation. To achieve this state of grace, the student has slowly moved ever away from the unholy posture of layman, upward to the sanctified status of the professional, being divested of worldly care and attributes along the way. The result: "the true professional", "the finished product", "the outcome of the system".'

This approach to the study of professional socialization, then, entails a focus upon the students' experiences within the context of the institutionalized body which nurtures and keeps the profession's knowledge and culture.

An alternative to the functionalist approach to the study of trainee doctors was taken by Becker (1961) and his fellow researchers. Becker *et al.* adopted an interactionist approach which focuses upon the students' behaviour rather than the professional role. The interactionists start from the premise that students will react to the education process which they experience and that they will negotiate their role and determine their actions accordingly. Central to the interactionists' work is the notion of a 'student culture' which develops as a distinctive subculture within the medical school. They use culture in an anthropological sense to mean: 'a body of ideas and practices considered to support each other and expected to support each other by members of the same group of people' (Becker *et al.* 1961:436). The perspectives developed by the students in order to 'get through' medical school, taken together form the 'student culture'.

'They develop ways of acting, studying and working which make it possible for them to achieve the goal in the situation they had defined. Similarly, the students in their clinical years saw the situation as one in which the goal of learning what was necessary for the practice of medicine might be interfered with by the structure of the hospital and by the necessity of making a good impression on the faculty. As they came into contact with clinical medicine they developed new goals that were more specific than those that they had had before.'

(Becker *et al.* 1961:436)

Becker *et al.*, then, focused their attention upon how students got through medical school, how they 'made out'. Their analysis is therefore much more to do with how students negotiate their way through the professional socialization and, as such, play a vital part in it. As they put it:

> 'He [the student] adapts his behavior to the situation as he sees it, ignoring possible lines of action which appear pre-ordained to fail or unworkable, discarding those which may cause conflict – in short, choosing the action which seems reasonable and expedient.'
>
> (Becker *et al.* 1961:442)

Merton and his associates saw the student in terms of 'junior colleague', whereas Becker *et al.* saw him merely as a student, indeed they point out at length that:

> 'students do not take on a professional role while they are students, largely because the system they operate in does not allow them to do so. They are not doctors and the recurring experiences of being denied responsibility make it perfectly clear to them that they are not.'
>
> (Becker *et al.*1961:420)

Olesen and Whittaker (1968) in their important work on student nurses abandoned the 'empty vessels to be filled' approach to occupational socialization. They say that their study is 'about becoming'. In many ways their work reflects the findings of Becker *et al.* in *Boys in White* (1961). This is particularly true in their discussion of 'studentmanship', which was the term they used for the student nurses' strategies for success and survival. 'Studentmanship' is similar to the 'student culture' which Becker *et al.* describe among the medical students in Kansas. Both constructs describe how students develop perspectives on their day-to-day work which allow them to 'get through' and achieve their long-term goals. Olesen and Whittaker's study is best described by their own final remarks on the study: 'the workable model for study of students in the professions is the model of the student as an active, choice-making factor in his own socialization' (Olesen and Whittaker 1968:300). Merton (1957:278) summed up the process of socialization thus: 'the process by which people selectively acquire the values and attitudes, the interests, skills and knowledge

– in short the culture – current in the groups of which they are or seek to become, a member.' Merton suggests that socialization takes place primarily through social interaction with people who are significant for the individual, namely the staff of the medical school, fellow students, and other hospital personnel. In the case of the student nurses in this study, the permanent staff, trained and untrained, and other student nurses appear to have been the significant people in this respect.

Miller (1970:118), again in connection with medical students, says that:

> 'Newcomers in any social situation go through an initial process of learning the ropes: finding out who the other people in that situation are, where they are located, what they do, what they expect the newcomer to do, and how they want him to do it. We seldom dignify this process by calling it learning.'

This kind of 'learning the ropes' experience is exactly the activity upon which the interactionist focuses. The students I interviewed described how the permanent staff on the wards made clear to them what was expected of them as student nurses. The processes involved in finding out about and reacting to these expectations is the main concern here.

Before examining the occupational socialization of the student nurse it is necessary first to ask how the students perceived both the nursing role and its acquisition. The question of how the students acquired the role of the registered nurse turned out to be rather more readily answered than how they perceived the role.

The students' notion of 'nurse'

I asked the students to tell me what they thought a nurse should be. This question was not often introduced head on, rather it emerged during the discussion of the ideal or the stereotype nurse. Some of the students said that they had been surprised to find what nursing was like. It was somewhat different from what they expected, yet they found it difficult to describe what they *had* expected. So whilst the data concerning the students' image of an ideal nurse are by no means exhaustive, they provide a useful introduction to the business of 'learning the rules'.

One student typified the position of many when she talked

about the 'student mould' into which the staff expected the students to fit.

STUDENT: Well I'd like to be able to sometimes do things that you want to do in the ward, not to have everything, you know, got to just fall into the mould all the time, that a student should be and just do that (. . .).[1]

KM: So what's the student nurse mould that you say you are supposed to fit in?

STUDENT: Just sort of doing what you are told and sort of not questioning. I sometimes feel the nurses, the student nurses, who do that are much happier – just looking round at them – they are much happier because they don't create any problems and they don't get into trouble: not that I have I've always been very lucky. But they don't have so many problems, they just go puppet-like about their work and don't question anything, I don't understand it. If you don't understand why you are doing a thing, I don't see the point of doing it.

This student recognized the stereotype student nurse image when she said that they 'fall into the mould'. The students suggested that the permanent staff on the wards did not regard them as individuals, rather, as a workforce made up of different grades of nurse. Thus, so long as a ward has its complement of junior and senior students slotted into the available spaces, the students need not be thought of as individuals. Indeed as the student quoted above says, some students find life easier if they fit unquestioningly into their slot. If the students' description of the attitude of the permanent staff is accurate, it is also perhaps not too surprising. The attitude which the students claim the permanent staff adopt is, it could be argued, a reasonable response to the labour situation which confronts them. The trained staff are responsible for achieving nursing work on the ward and are accountable to patients, nursing management, and medical staff for the standard of care on the ward. Thus, whilst the students might find the permanent staff's reaction to their presence on the ward annoying, and so describe it in terms of a complaint against the staff, it is, from

[1] I have used (. . .) to indicate where words have been omitted and . . . for pauses.

the viewpoint of the ward staff, a rational response to the fact of mobile student labour.

Students had to find ways of coming to terms with being part of the workforce. The feeling of not knowing what to do or how to behave in hospital was common to many of the students. The following extract, which is part of a discussion concerned with feeling more at home in the hospital, illustrates the point:

STUDENT: I don't know, you are just more relaxed in the environment, I think. Because when I first started off . . . maybe because you don't know the ward and you don't know how to react in a hospital, you get used to it, even if it is a new ward, just because you know what the hospital is like or you have worked there before, or even you know the kind of routine of most wards. I think you relax more yourself and it makes it easier to talk to somebody, whereas if you are a stranger yourself, it's slightly harder.

KM: You said that you didn't know how to react in a hospital, how have you learned to do that?

STUDENT: I don't really know, I suppose it's just come from experience; before I was petrified of hospitals, even if I go to see someone in a hospital I'm quite scared, but I think when you work there . . . if I was in hospital myself I'd be slightly nervous but because I'm working there I know how to go about it, you're more relaxed (. . .). You copy the older nurses in a lot of things you do, how you explain things and how you listen to a patient. I think you copy a lot of people, I suppose it must be from copying other people – but to behave as a nurse, I don't think anybody knows how to do that. You don't imagine yourself as a nurse on a ward, you know you are a nurse but . . . not many people think of it at the time.

KM: You mean the public image of the nurse, you don't think of yourself as . . .

STUDENT: Yes, the kind of Florence Nightingale thing. Nursing is not what I thought it would be (. . .) it wasn't what I'd gone in to. You just kind of imagine something and it's not what it's like so you don't imagine what you're doing is nursing . . . doesn't follow story books you read when you are younger.

KM: Can you say what you expected?

STUDENT: Can't really, just imagined it all different. I think it is
            very much academic, you really have to be intelligent
            to be a nurse which I think is very wrong. Because
            there are a lot of good nurses that aren't intelligent, but
            people who are kind, know how to handle people and
            relax them (. . .).

This student, along with many I spoke to, talks about copying
other nurses, often it was other students' behaviour that they
copied. Interestingly the student quoted above still maintains the
notion that there is a way which is acceptable for a nurse to behave;
even though she does not claim to know what it is.

The idea of a public image of the nurse was popular with the
students. They said that the patients have preconceived ideas about
how nurses should behave and what they should be like. The
image that the patient has of the nurse was often thought to be
quite important for the student nurse's self-esteem. If the patient
thought that the nurse looked competent and knowledgeable then
the students said that they were more likely to feel competent. As
in the case of the student quoted above, who had a rather romantic
notion of nursing, many students did not feel ready for what they
encountered in nursing. For instance, the question of whether
nursing is too academic or not sufficiently so, was raised several
times by the students.

Occupational socialization

Bucher and Stelling (1977) emphasize the importance of the
mastery of skills by the trainee. They argue that until there is a sense
of the skills involved in the work being mastered, the students
cannot develop a commitment to nor identify with the profession
that they are preparing to join. 'Until one is actually involved in
doing the work of the field, it is difficult to demonstrate for oneself,
or to others, that one has acquired the required skills and
knowledge' (1977:267). Bucher and Stelling stress the primacy of
role-playing activity. If it is to result in a sense of mastery, though,
role-playing activities 'must involve some degree of autonomy
and responsibility on the part of the trainee; the trainee must, at
least, perceive that he or she is acting independently, and has the
responsibility for those actions' (1977:267).

In describing their experiences on the wards, the students I interviewed revealed themselves to be so preoccupied with getting by on a day-to-day basis, that they had little time to think of how they might learn to do the work of qualified nurses. The notion that anticipatory socialization might occur during the three years spent as a student does not appear to be particularly useful in the light of the students' description of their experience. Following Olesen and Whittaker (1968) and Becker *et al.* (1961), it seems reasonable to suppose that the students concern themselves with adapting to current situations, rather than preparing to take on the role of qualified nurse at some future date.

The students were introduced to the expectations attached to their role almost as soon as they began to work on the wards. The permanent staff, as we have said, wasted no time in letting the students know that they were expected to 'pull their weight' and to 'get through the work' in as short a time as possible. The students spoke of the speed with which they were expected to work on the wards. This did not compare with the ways they had been taught in college. The way in which the students spoke of the need for speed demonstrates just how real they found the pressures from the permanent staff to conform. Even though the students knew that what they had been taught in the college was at odds with the practice on the wards, they were prepared to justify the hurried approach to ward nursing in the same terms used by the ward staff. This was exemplified by one student during a discussion about the lack of time for the sister to teach on a busy ward:

KM: And you are left to find out for yourself in the wards where they are under-staffed and so they don't have time to teach.

STUDENT: Yes, fair enough in geriatrics, that's where you can really learn your basic nursing care, in the care of elderly patients you have the time to take time with a back round [see p. 33] and do the full ward in an hour and a half because there's nothing much doing in geriatrics. Whereas, if you go up from geriatrics to a busy surgical ward, the junior nurses still take the amount of time to do a back round, which you can't do if you have got a busy theatre list, you're admitting emergency patients and they [the juniors] are needed for somewhere else to do another job and are still doing

a back round. It's just not on (. . .). It's adaptability,
you've got to adapt to your ward situation where you
can take your time and where you can't (. . .).

KM: So the difference you are talking about, is the speed
with which you do the back round, not that you do
anything different, is that right?

STUDENT: It's the speed. You can take your time in geriatric
wards, or wards that aren't busy.

This student had not only adopted the permanent staff's rhetoric
and explanations for the speed of work, but she also supported the
idea, and was prepared to uphold it in front of the junior nurses. In
a sense, she can be said to have been fully socialized into the nurse
role in accordance with the wishes of the permanent staff. She had
not only taken over their attitudes towards the work, but was
prepared to hand them on to other students.

Not all students were so prepared to go along with the notion
that nursing at speed was not only necessary, but a good thing. The
following extract puts this alternative viewpoint.

STUDENT: (. . .) I've been told it takes seven minutes to do a bed
bath. If they are not finished by 10 am, you are falling
behind. We should be allowed to do things in the time
they take to do. I've been on wards where I suddenly
think, 'I'm being slow', there mightn't be any other
pressures or other things to do, but I take time because
that's the way the ward is going.

KM: The sorts of pressures you are talking about, these are
hard to define in some ways aren't they? For example,
you could have a sister who says you must be done by
10 am, and you still have two legs and a bottom to do.
But again, even if there isn't a sister who is hurrying
you up do you sometimes feel like you said just then –
'I'm being slow'? What is it that's pushing you then?

STUDENT: An alarm clock inside, probably just your own personal feeling of what others think of you.

KM: This comes back to what you said earlier about 'the
nurse' would do it quickly.

STUDENT: Yes, you hear some nurses are slow. They may be, it
doesn't mean she can't be a good nurse. I've seen these
mad machine nurses, I'm thinking of one now, it's like
a production line. The staff nurse recently started on a

medical ward, a very easy going ward, you feel free to
do your work properly. I'd do bathing with her, I'm
not a fast bather – what's the point – bathing with her
was like a competition. Like one of these old films
speeded up. The patient may be chatting away and her
not listening to a word, saying 'yes' and 'no' maybe but
she was totally within herself. I felt she was working to
make it look good in the front office.

The above extract illustrates several interesting points from the
data. This student did not value speed, indeed she could not see any
patient benefits to be gained from working at such a pace.
However, she clearly recognized that it was a trait which created a
good impression in some nursing circles. She suggested, for
example, that the 'mad machine' staff nurse was only doing the
amount of work that she did in order to impress the nursing
hierarchy, the 'front office'. This student had worked in wards
where, she felt, the timetabling of the care was strict, even going so
far as to have some notional time limit for bed baths. Yet she could
still feel pressurized into hurrying in her work when there was not
any overt pressure being brought to bear. The idea of some kind of
internalized monitor, the 'alarm clock' inside her, was raised in one
way or another by a few of the students. It was mentioned
sometimes in the context of junior and senior student nurse
behaviour. A third year student claimed that she had become much
more likely to defend her behaviour as a senior student than she
might have been at the start of her training. I pursued the point
about the alarm clock.

KM: Do you find there is a sort of feeling in nursing that if
you are fast, you are good, it doesn't matter how you
do it so long as you get it done by . . .?

STUDENT: Yes, there is a feeling, I don't think it is necessarily
right, but there is. I mean everybody likes being on
with staff nurse who is going to have the ward all in
order; and sister is going to come on and everything is
going to be done, towels are not on radiators, soap not
wet in the lockers and clothes not hanging out of the
doors – it doesn't really make that much difference to
patient care you know! Everybody likes, I mean it's
just the usually accepted way, the ward has got to be
tidy (. . .).

KM: In some of these interviews we have talked about this kind of thing, and it's often quite difficult to pinpoint why people feel like that, it's not necessarily that someone keeps saying 'you must be quick' – but the students say they feel that they are looking over their shoulder all the time and think 'I've been in here a long time, I wish this patient would hurry up'.

STUDENT: Yes you do, you do.

KM: And I wonder where that comes from? There is a sort of stereotype of the nurse that she should work fast.

STUDENT: I think, well there seems to be, and the more junior you are the more I used to try to fit into that category. But now I turn round when somebody says 'what have you been doing in there?' I still keep the speed up to get as much done as I possibly can, if I've been in for a long time, and, say, a patient starts crying or something, you can't just say 'oh shut up' – you really can't say that. You say so and so is upset, so I stayed rather a long time in there and that's that. I've got to the point where it really doesn't bother me, if someone says, 'you've been in there for ages' – I just say 'too bad'.

The comments of the last student demonstrate, not only how the student nurse might become more adept at defending her own behaviour as she becomes more senior, but also, and more importantly, that the need for such defence clearly exists. Her description of the tidy ward in which everyone likes to work and the idea that 'speed' somehow equates with 'good' nursing exemplify the feeling, among the student nurses, that such a thing as an 'ideal' nurse, or at least 'ideal nursing' exists, if only in the form of some distant grail.

Unwritten rules

The students seemed to be describing a code, or set of rules which, if followed, would allow them to present the kind of behaviour that the trained staff found acceptable. The students, by following these rules, were able to display a mastery of nursing work as it is carried out on the wards. I have described these rules as 'unwritten' because, although they were clearly very powerful, the students had difficulty in pinpointing exactly where they were to be found.

For example, the students found it difficult to explain where the idea that nursing work should be done quickly came from. These rules were not overt, rather they were made known and enforced by more subtle means. Stated briefly, the 'unwritten rules' said that students should work quickly and 'pull their weight' in doing a fair share of the work. Moreover, if there was no work to be done they should endeavour to 'look busy' in order to preserve the overall atmosphere of activity and efficiency. The concepts of 'talking versus working' and 'looking busy' are related to the idea of social control, taken together they shed some light on the notion of occupational socialization in nursing.

As the notion of the 'unwritten rule' began to emerge as a dimension of the socialization category, I asked one student in the course of a discussion of ward organization:

KM: Is there an unspoken set of rules . . .
STUDENT: Yes.
KM: . . . of the way you are meant to behave in a hospital?
STUDENT: Very definitely, yes I think there is.
KM: How do you feel them if you don't hear . . .
STUDENT: Just from the looks you get, if things are out of place they just look at you, just find out not from asking anybody, its just there somehow, you just know it – that's accepted and that's it. People sometimes emit it so strongly that you just know that you don't do that sort of thing.
KM: A little bit like doing everything in a hurry.
STUDENT: Everyone normally works in a hurry, so you had better not do anything else.

This student put into words the way in which the unwritten rules are enforced. The fact that the student felt that all the staff needed to do was to give a 'look' in order to ensure that the student toes the line, indicates that there is a fairly clear and universal understanding within the wards of the expectations associated with the role of the student nurse.

The students talked of the need to demonstrate that they were 'doing well on the ward', and their surest way of achieving this was to 'pull their weight'. Students could recognize instances when another student or a member of the trained staff was not doing their fair share of the work. The extract below illustrates this point:

STUDENT: You can maybe have one staff nurse or one enrolled
            nurse that feels themselves above everyone (. . .) she
            spends half the time in the office, before we had even
            had report she'd be writing out the menu cards while
            we are trying to give out breakfasts, then rush into
            report and then rush out again to get them all to the
            toilet (. . .). It was resented by everyone on that ward,
            just one particular nurse. On the other hand, she was
            the one who did a lot of caring. She didn't do much of
            the hard grind stuff, but if there was someone seriously
            ill, she would sit with them, which is important. On
            the other hand, people would say 'why is she just
            sitting there when we have all this to do?' You have
            your priorities, but she never pulled her weight
            whether there was something that needed done or not
            (. . .). Mucking about with forms, discharge papers,
            files, etc. when there was work to be done. She was the
            only one, most of the staff were in there with their
            sleeves rolled up just the same as us.

Here the student nurse took exception to the way that a member of
the permanent staff was not 'pulling her weight'. It is interesting to
note that 'pulling her weight' clearly referred to physical work.
The student recognized the care which the nurse in question give
to seriously ill patients, but felt, nevertheless, that the 'hard grind'
should be shared by all. The overriding impression that I gained
from these discussions was, once again, that nursing work is hard
and heavy work to be got through. Because of this, students,
qualified staff, and auxiliaries alike are expected to join in and 'get
through'. If we accept that this is how the work is viewed by the
students, a suggestion which is supported by Clarke (1978), it is not
surprising that there is an elaborate system of moral pressure and
social control operating in order to ensure that the work is shared.
The 'unwritten rules' are unwritten because to voice them or
formalize them would necessitate the open recognition of nursing
in these 'workload' terms. Terms which go against the general tide
of caring and professional ideals. Students or qualified staff who do
not 'pull their weight' and do a fair day's work can be seen to be
letting the side down, or not playing fair.

Unwritten rule: 'talking isn't working'

If such a system of social control as the students describe is to work, the expectations and sanctions must be clear to those involved. The data suggest that talking to patients is an important feature in this control. The students often commented that the permanent staff did not recognize talking with patients as nursing work. The whole issue of talking versus working became an important one in the development of this category. The following extract makes the point:

STUDENT: Sometimes people in charge of the ward object, they like you to work all the time, tend to forget that you should go and speak to patients, if they see you stand and talk, they tend to think you are skiving – just not pulling your weight.

KM: You used the word work – is talking working as far as you are concerned?

STUDENT: Yes, but it's just seen as being lazy, not pulling your weight, you get sent to clean cupboards and things.

As it has been said, the main 'unwritten rule' is that the students should 'pull their weight'. According to the students one of the prime ways of indicating that they were not doing this, as far as the trained staff were concerned, was by talking to patients. Thus, even if there was little work to do, it was, generally speaking, more acceptable to try to 'look busy' than to demonstrate a lack of work by talking with the patients. This argument is posed rather sharply, and is necessarily simplified, in order to make the point. Not all wards operated such a clear-cut system of ensuring that students pulled their weight. Some ward sisters, the students said, encouraged them to talk with patients whilst others 'allowed' them to. Interestingly the use of the word 'allowed' in this context, whilst indicating a more liberal approach to nursing work, still belies the fact that the students have internalized the idea that physical work is what nursing is about.

One student said that if she got on well with the ward sister she could feel more relaxed in a ward.

KM: Does this affect your relationship with the patients, do you think?

STUDENT: I think so, because if you are sort of frightened of the sister you're probably frightened to go up and talk to patients because she'll think, you know, that you're not getting on with your work. But I think also I found with the younger ones [sisters], who realize that you have to talk to the patients, sort of understand them, and I mean, it might not look very good if a nurse is sitting down by someone's bed, she looks as if she's not doing anything, just sitting there having a blether, but I think it's very important for the patient rather than just seeing these nurses rushing up and down all the time and not bothering with them.

This extract demonstrates the ambivalence which the students felt towards talking with patients. They knew at one level that it was a good thing for the patients and, indeed, an essential part of nursing. Yet, the rhetoric they used suggested that they had internalized the prevailing dictum of work before talk.

Another student, in describing how a ward sister could show her care for patients, said:

STUDENT: (. . .) she would go up and talk to patients and tell nurses to go and talk to patients rather than have them *looking* like they are busy. When I first went into nursing the big thing was for every nurse to look like she was doing something, even if she wasn't, she'd look like she was doing something. I find some other sisters just don't believe that they want you to talk to patients – one way of showing they care. There's a lot of feedback on those wards.

KM: From?

STUDENT: From the students to senior staff.

KM: Why do you think that is, because the . . .

STUDENT: Well, because the students are talking to the patients and getting more information. Probably because on those wards the sisters aren't like – from the old school – they are very friendly (. . .) one sister will not forbid you but you didn't get to talk to the patients unless you were actually doing something for the patient at the time. Whereas, on another ward in a quiet spell you could go and sit down and talk to your patient and nothing would be said, in fact, you'd probably be

thought of as a valuable member of staff (. . .) could
help in your nursing care.

This student puts forward a practical reason for talking with
patients when she mentions feedback. Her rationale for talking
with patients is interesting in that she redefines it as a useful part of
nursing, which can provide information for the senior staff and
'help in the nursing care'. In a sense, she legitimates talking in terms
of its function and so equates it with other forms of nursing work.
She then goes so far as to say that by talking to patients the students
can be seen as valuable members of the ward staff, because of the
information which they gather whilst talking.

Another student put forward a positive reason for talking with
patients when she said that if a student did not talk with patients it
might be suggested, in her ward assessment, that she lacked
confidence. Talking with patients was considered by the students
to be a possible sign that they were not pulling their weight and
consequently creating a poor impression with the permanent staff.
This latter point is of importance to the students as they receive an
assessment from each ward which counts towards their professional registration. Thus, apart from the fact that the students' day-
to-day life on the wards was made more comfortable if they
obeyed the 'unwritten rules', they had good reason to wish to
create a favourable impression, namely their ward report.

Unwritten rule: 'looking busy'

The ward report and the 'looks' given by the permanent staff are
not the only means of ensuring that the 'unwritten rules' are
obeyed. The other students form a source of social pressure as
described by this student. Again, the discussion centred around the
key factor, talking with patients.

KM: You said you wanted to create a good impression
(. . .). There seems to be a general idea of what a good
nurse is.

STUDENT: Uh huh.

KM: The image of a bustling efficient nurse who never has
time to stop (. . .). Where do you get that image from?
There seem to be things that nurses do that aren't quite
sensible, like looking busy all the time, finding things
to do.

STUDENT: There is a feeling in the ward that you can't sit down
            and chat to a patient and no matter if a staff nurse or
            ward sister says 'Yes go and chat to patients, it's
            alright', you've got this thing inside you that says 'no,
            no, I should be going to do this' – which is very bad, I
            don't know where it is from (. . .). In first year
            whenever I spoke to a patient I always stood up, never
            sat down, thought sister would think I'm being lazy or
            something. Which is ridiculous, if a nurse is always
            standing up and the patient always lying down, it
            hardly puts the patient at ease (. . .).

KM: (. . .) When you think someone might think you're
            lazy, is there any pressure from the other staff, or even
            your fellow students – someone has an easy day and
            I've done all the work feeling.

STUDENT: Yes, I suppose there is, if you're sitting chatting to
            someone and your fellow student goes into the sluice,
            you keep on thinking I wonder what she is doing, I
            wonder what she is stocking up or cleaning. You feel
            you should be helping her with hard work – it's OK if
            two of you are standing talking, but then a patient is
            not so much at ease with two people – better one to one
            (. . .). It is true if your friend is working you should be
            helping her and not sitting down chatting to a patient.
            You feel that chatting to a patient is not working, it is
            more a pleasure. I think that is where the feeling is from
            (. . .). Yet each nurse knows that to talk to a patient is
            very important.

Another student felt that it should not be necessary to 'look busy'
when there was nothing to do.

STUDENT: If you've got maybe say half an hour and all the work's
            done, you know, there is nothing really to do, well
            most people, nurses in training, they just want to go
            and talk to patients or something whereas, you know,
            the sister comes in and she'll make you scrub out the
            sluices, say, or the treatment room, which is a complete
            waste of time, it's getting scrubbed about ten times a
            day, you know, and she's just doing that for the sake of,
            you know, giving you something to do. It's a waste of

time (. . .). I mean, if all the work is done, I don't see any harm in doing what you want to do. You know, like talking to patients, or even studying. I mean, you get exams and that, when there's not a lot of work to do in the ward, there's no reason why you couldn't study, but you know they make you either stand about, empty buckets, or something (. . .). If there's nothing to do, you know, you should be allowed to study or talk to patients instead of trying to look busy, I mean this is ridiculous, because everybody knows that you're just trying to look busy. I mean even when visitors come in they say, 'is this you trying to look busy'. Well, I mean they must have some weird ideas about what nurses do, you know, because when they see you, you're always sort of hanging about looking for something to do, because at visiting times there is not a lot you can do.

KM: That's strange because earlier you said that the patients tend to think, and I would agree, because I've seen it too, think you're always too busy. How do you find that to cope with, when you have got spare time, just to go and talk to patients? How do you feel about that?

STUDENT: Most of the time I suppose you are too busy but I think patients conjure up this image that nurses are too busy, you can't interrupt them because, I suppose, it is just force of habit you're always rushing about and I think there is so much said about nurses and doctors you know how they are always busy, so much to do and I don't think they realize that, I mean you know, you're not like that all the time because, I mean, there's always times that you're not busy and there's not a lot to do.

This student put forward concrete suggestions for legitimate activities, which students could engage in, when there is no 'work' to do. She suggests that the 'looking busy' tactic does not even convince the visitors and furthermore, it blocks the patients' access to the nurse. On these grounds she favours study time or talking to patients as legitimate activities when physical nursing work is done.

Unwritten rules and social control

The 'unwritten rules' which deem that the students should 'pull their weight', work quickly and 'look busy', even when there is little or nothing to do, are enforced by various sanctions available to the workforce on the ward. The ward sister has, as her ultimate sanction, the students' ward reports. The other permanent staff, and indeed the students themselves, resort to group pressures and social controls of a more subtle nature.

The ways in which nursing behaviour can be controlled and managed have been described in various ways by researchers. Pill's (1970) accounts of the work of nurses on children's wards draw upon Goffman's (1959) analyses in *The Presentation of Self in Everyday Life*. Pill applies his notion that there are particular aspects of work which are accentuated in the presence of other people and other, less creditable, aspects which are suppressed.

> 'One of the most popular conceptions about the role of the nurse is that she is continually busy even overworked. This theme cropped up constantly in the interviews at home with mothers before the child went into hospital, when asked what they thought about unrestricted visiting. . . . [Mothers] mentioned that the staff had a lot to do and their fear of 'being in the way'. The latter remark indicates an implicit recognition that the ward is somehow the nurses' territory, a feeling that is certainly shared by the nurses. The mothers are, following Goffman's interesting analysis "outsiders" trespassing on the nurses' place of work. The introduction of unrestricted visiting means that the nurses are or likely to be, under observation the whole day by "outsiders"; who will therefore be in a good position to see exactly what and how much the nurses do.'
>
> (Pill in Stacey *et al.* 1970:118–20)

Pill found a similar activity to the 'looking busy' tactics described by the students in this study; she describes this as 'make work'. She also describes the ways in which the nurses achieved the impression of a busy ward. 'The nurse also quite frequently disappears whilst parents are in the ward . . . reappearing at intervals to glance round briefly. This fosters the impression of activity' (1970:120). In the context of unrestricted visiting, Pill suggested that the nurses found difficulty in determining what behaviour was appropriate in terms of 'on stage behaviour' in the 'front regions' and relaxed behaviour in the 'back regions'. The nurses' behaviour, described by Pill, supports the notion that 'looking busy' is a tactic employed on hospital wards. The students I interviewed appreciated that they engaged in 'front region' behaviour much of the time, yet could not see why 'back room' behaviour could not be carried out on the wards. (For instance, the student who thought that private study should be an acceptable student activity on the ward.)

It is interesting to note that students often felt better about talking to a patient if they could see another student doing so too. They described an implicit feeling of guilt which is attached to sitting and talking when they cannot be sure what the other students are doing. This feeling of unease can probably be explained in terms of the students feeling that they might be letting the side down on two possible counts. Firstly, there might actually be some work to do, in which case they are not 'pulling their weight'. Secondly, although there is no actual work to do, the other students may be engaging in the 'looking busy' tactic. The students who are talking with patients are demonstrating, by the very act of talking, that they are not working. Not only are they not working, but they are not prepared to adopt the 'look busy' tactics which support the efficient nurse front dictated by the 'unwritten rules' of the wards.

The social pressures which students described, from both fellow students and permanent staff, ensure that the overall pace and 'output' of work remains constant. There is an extensive literature in industrial sociology which describes what has been called 'restriction of output' (Lupton 1963; Roy 1952, 1954). These studies are essentially concerned with reasons behind the gap between expected and actual output from industrial machine shops. The workers engaged in manipulation of the piecework scheme. Roy (1954) concluded that workers behaved as they did in order to protect their economic position. The restrictive behaviour of the workers was aimed at establishing some control over the working situation and earnings. This power struggle is best described by one of Roy's informants:

'What do you suppose would happen if I turned in $1.25 an hour on these pump bodies?'

'Turned in? You mean if you actually did the work?'

'I mean if I actually did the work and turned it in.'

'They'd have to pay you wouldn't they? Isn't that the agreement?'

'Yes, they'd pay me once! Don't you know that if I turned in $1.50 an hour on these pump bodies tonight the whole God-damned Methods Department would be down here tomorrow? And they'd re-time this job so quick it would make your head swim! And when they re-timed it they'd cut the price in half and I'd be working for 85 cents an hour instead of $1.25!'

The general impression gained from these studies is that as soon as a worker increases his production, the management takes advantage of it, by cutting the piecework rate. In the case of nursing, it could be argued that the nurses have to appear to be fully occupied throughout their spell of duty, otherwise the administrators responsible for allocation of staff might move them to a busier area of the hospital. The comments made by managers from the commercial sector about the over-staffing of hospital wards at the changeover of shifts period provide a similar example of an inappropriate match of workstyle and the task in hand (Griffiths 1983). So long as talking is not thought to constitute working, it adds to the time which the nurses 'waste'. The 'looking busy' tactics could, therefore, be compared with the 'time wasting' or 'loafing' which the machine shop workers had to engage in so that they could appear to be working as fast as the job was 'timed', without actually achieving the required output. The socialization of new machine shop workers described by Roy (1952, 1954) is similar to the descriptions that I heard from the students in this study. The staff, qualified and unqualified, and other students soon make the newcomer aware both of how much work she must do, and how busy she should appear whilst doing it.

The words one student used to describe the work–talk dichotomy, namely 'work versus pleasure', suggest an extremely puritanical view of what nursing should be like. This conception of talking versus working upholds the idea that nursing work is to be got through, rather than to be enjoyed along the way. The notion that talking is not working is important on two counts. First, the students are placed under some considerable stress if they feel that the patient wants to talk, yet they are equally aware of a strong opposing pull to get the work done. Second, if the general ethos on the wards is that talking can only take place once the work is done, the possibility of putting into practice the much vaunted individualized care, which must depend upon communication, becomes remote.

Because nursing is construed as work to be done, a tension is produced between the ideal form of nursing and its operationalized form, which is practised on the wards. The operationalized form of nursing is hard to fault as it provides an efficient means of 'getting through' on a busy ward. Clearly, as these data suggest, the work then talk dictum makes a degree of sense. Student nurses are caught in this tension. They receive the idealized notions about nursing from the college and experience social pressures on the ward which urge them to set that aside and adopt the 'get the work done' *modus operandi* of the wards.

The question of occupational socialization is particularly interesting in the case of nursing. The early work concerned with medical students (Merton 1957) took the conventional view of socialization when the behaviour of the medical students was seen to be controlled and shaped by the medical faculty, which acts as an agent of the medical profession. The students gradually acquire the professional culture and become fully fledged professionals. Later work by Becker *et al.* (1961) suggested the students had much more of a part to play in their socialization, and indeed saw the whole process in terms of a negotiation of behaviour between student and professionals. The exponents of this reaction model of occupational socialization do not consider that the attitudes and behaviour learned during professional education are the major influences on the future behaviour of the students. Becker *et al.* discovered that the students' major preoccupation had to do with short term goals of meeting the requirements of the curriculum, rather than longer term goals of achieving professional status. The reaction approach to socialization appears to be more fitting to student nurses than the induction approach; moreover, it is debatable whether the socialization of the student nurse can be said to be a professional socialization, or merely 'on the job' training, which produces functioning nurses. We shall return to this theme.

Now that we have seen how the students learn to function on the wards, we are ready to move on to look, in some detail, at how nursing work is achieved and organized on the wards.

2

GETTING THE WORK DONE

In learning to 'pass' as nurses on the wards, the students are made very much aware of the fact that the main business of the ward is to get through the nursing work. In the last chapter we saw how the students were encouraged by the permanent staff to go about this nursing work in such a way that they always seem to have enough to do. Clearly the students had to be able to do rather more than simply look busy. They had to gain an understanding of how nursing work was accomplished on the wards and to determine what their part in that work should be. This chapter, then, is concerned with the students' accounts of the work and its organization on hospital wards. Nurses frequently talk in terms of 'running the ward', when they describe the work of caring for patients in hospital. The students I interviewed described different styles of management which they encountered, styles of management directed in one way or another towards 'running the ward'. The category 'getting the work done' is explored in this chapter by looking at 'routines' and the different means of supervision employed by the ward sister.[1] The main focus is upon how the students do their nursing work on the wards and how the ward organization is perceived by the student nurse.

In describing the constraints of the ward from the students' viewpoint this account is not intended to present a deterministic explanation of the students' social world. The students, as adults, are able to negotiate, to an extent, their relationship with the prevailing structure and thus come to some working relationship within this. Whilst it must be said that some elements of the

---

[1] 'Ward sister' is the term used as the students were describing women. For convenience 'ward sister' is used throughout the text when reference is made to the charge nurse role.

hospital social structure are less tractable than others, the students do have a certain amount of manoeuvring room.

One of my underlying interests in this study had to do with how nursing work organization, at ward level, impinges on the students. During the interviews the issue of ward organization was often raised by the students; where this was not the case, I introduced the topic, in broad terms, by asking how nursing care was organized on the wards on which the student had worked. The question of how ward work is organized invariably led to comments about 'getting the work done' and 'getting the ward cleared'. Clarke (1978) in a paper entitled 'Getting Through the Work' described nurses' attitudes towards work in the long-stay geriatric wards of a psychiatric hospital. The category, 'getting the work done', as it is developed here relies heavily upon Clarke's work.

Routine and running the ward

When asked how work was organized on the different wards, the students commonly said that there were marked differences between the wards. However, as they went on to describe these it became clear that there were some factors common to most wards. The following extracts serve to illustrate some of the points.

STUDENT: I think the type of nursing depends on the staff that are there all the time.

KM: The permanent staff on the ward.

STUDENT: Huh huh, they've got an awful lot of influence on, well, the way the ward is run. Some wards you have to do certain things and therefore that affects the way you nurse.

KM: Can you give any examples – what kind of things?

STUDENT: Back rounds, especially pressure areas, well any sort of pressure areas, even on the same ward you get the different staff . . . say the SENs do one thing one way and the sister likes to do it another. Sometimes it's very confusing (. . .).

KM: Yes, how do you find that to work with, if you've got to keep changing in one ward it must be difficult.

STUDENT: It's very difficult because, like I say, you've got to remember who's on [duty]; in one ward I was on if the sister was on you didn't make the beds until after dinner; if the other staff were on [i.e. in charge] you'd make the beds.

Another student distinguished between different types of ward, but then went on to describe individual characteristics of the ward sister.

KM: Do you find the ways the different sisters run their wards similar, or do you find quite a change from one to another?

STUDENT: Yes, they are quite different, you can't really compare medical with surgical; you have to compare one surgical ward with another, basically the same type of patients (. . .). I find the attitude of the ward sister does make a difference. There is one ward where the sister got in a flap about everything, if on an early shift, she stayed on until 7 pm [instead of 4.30 pm] to see if you are alright; if a student's in charge she was 'phoning all the time saying have you done this, etc. That set a 'guddly' [muddled, chaotic] attitude on the ward, you never got on. Others are down to earth. The ones who work themselves are good; the ones that sit in the office, people resent them and don't work as well for her. If the ward sister mucks in, it makes a difference.

KM: Yes, that keeps cropping up; whether everyone should join in or not − how do you see that?

STUDENT: Definitely should, yes.

KM: Do you see the ward sister's role as different from the rest of the nurses or should she be the same?

STUDENT: No, fair enough, I know she has meetings, but if you are in wards that are really busy, like the ward sister in Ward A, she had time. I don't know how they get to know their patients if they are sitting in the office all day, just can't. I think there are fewer wards like that now, it is the older ones that do less.

KM: What about the way that the nursing work is organized. When you go on, how do you know what to do?

STUDENT: It's slightly different on each ward. Obviously the basic thing is in the morning they get a bath or bed bath,

> always drugs and charts to do. And by the time you
> have done a few years, or a few months, you know
> what has to be done, it's just the order it's done in that
> differs on different wards; you soon get into the way of
> it.

It seems that however much students learn in college about
individualized care and care plans for patients, as soon as they reach
the wards they are confronted with something rather different.
They spoke in terms of how the sister 'runs the ward' and whether
one sister's ways were like another's. The students had little
difficulty in perceiving the similarities and differences between the
wards, and as the student quoted above says, 'you soon get into the
way of it'.

The most likely explanation for this ability to 'get into the way
of it' lies in the fact that the nursing work is presented to the
students in the form of sets of routines. These routines can be
designed and established by the ward sister. In this way the sister
can be seen as the 'scientific manager' as expounded by Taylor
(1911) and elaborated upon by Braverman (1974). 'Scientific
management' is a work method introduced by Taylor towards the
end of the nineteenth century. Its general principle is to enable
work to be done by a less skilled workforce by means of having the
work supervised by those who are more qualified. Braverman
explains the system succinctly:

> 'Every step of the labor process is divorced, so far as possible,
> from special knowledge and training and reduced to simple
> labor. Meanwhile the relatively few people for whom special
> knowledge and training are reserved are freed, so far as possible,
> from the obligation of simple labor. In this way a structure is
> given to all labor process, that at its extreme polarises those
> whose time is infinitely valuable and those whose time is worth
> almost nothing.'
>
> (Braverman 1974:83)

The detail of the routines may vary. If for example, a nurse is
told to do a 'back round' she knows, from the similarities between
wards, that she has to undertake a 'round' of all the patients
attending to their skin care. The exact mechanics of how she goes
about this will vary from ward to ward, or, as we saw above, even

within the same ward depending upon who is on duty at the time. Interestingly, even though there have been great shifts in thinking about the care of patients' pressure areas and moves towards individualized care plans, the 'back round' has not lost its place in ward parlance and indeed reality.

The students also had strong ideas about how they liked to be directed in their work by the ward sister, some were quite clear about how care should be organized. In this connection, the students also commonly expressed the opinion that the trained staff should join in with the work. This gives us some indication of how nurses view 'work'; it is exemplified in the case of the student quoted above, the students equated 'work' with physically looking after patients. The ward sister who sits in her office is thought not to be working and to be out of touch with her patients. This is consistent with Clarke's findings: 'Both the interview and the observation material in this study suggest that the nurses' ideas of what properly constituted "work" involved expending physical energy' (Clarke 1978:77).

Styles of management on the ward

The students described the ways in which ward sisters organized the work of the ward. The students were interested in ward organization because it played a major part in determining how well they got on in their practical experience. The way in which the ward is 'run' is to a large extent dependent upon the management style of the ward sister. Two distinct types of management were distinguished by the students; one where the patient is the focus, commonly referred to as 'patient allocation,' and one where tasks and routines are the main features. The former style was less frequently encountered by the students. It also has to be said that where there was no managerial lead from the ward sister, alternative forms of organization emerged. The students frequently played a significant part in these alternative organizational modes.

Patient allocation is a way of organizing the delivery of nursing care in which each nurse is allocated one or more patients and is responsible for their care. The use of detailed care plans, in which written individualized instructions for the patient's care could be found, was the hallmark of a patient oriented style of management.

Clearly, several individual care plans could be combined and translated into routines in terms of the whole ward, and thus not all sisters who use care plans also use patient allocation.

Extracts from interviews presented below are offered in order to give some flavour of the styles of management of nursing work. We shall then discuss the implications, for students, of these styles.

KM: It just reminded me when you talked about starting the baths and the thought of them being worse than doing them. One of the things that people have talked about is 'getting through the work' and 'getting the ward cleared' and thinking in routines. Is it possible to think of individual patients once you get into the ward (. . .) or does it become a different way of going about things?

STUDENT: Ah hah, you see I personally feel that the ideal situation in hospital would be one nurse to two patients, or one nurse to one patient, depending how ill they were; and for them to be responsible for their total care. But on the other hand you see, when you do have the grades, different grades of staff, then that's like asking a first-year student to 'special' somebody; whereas usually specialling[1] would be done by a student further on. Somehow you have to divide it, how far they can go specialling that patient and how much responsibility is to be put on somebody else. So I think in a way the individual care doesn't happen quite so much, it is hard to do. Especially if you think of a ward with so many patients and it's their time to be bathed so you want to make all the beds; get them all to the toilet and all dressed, sat in the chair so you can give them all their cup of tea. You do start to start thinking like that rather than, now I must remember that Mrs So and So needs to have something or other done, and that she should really have it done before, or something like that. Or let's leave her to the last.

KM: The routine takes over.

[1] 'Specialling' refers to one nurse looking after one, usually seriously ill, patient.

…s, the routine, let's get it all done then we'll have …me. You never, I don't think you ever really achieve …hat, we'll have time – it just never comes. I think it could be more individual, just depends (. . .). Critically ill people, they are going to be bed bathed and so on anyway; so in that respect that's not so much the routine, that is individual care. Seems to depend on how severe their illness is.

This student describes lucidly how the patient centred style of management is the idealized form of care, and all too frequently not realized because of the pressure of numbers and time. The recourse to 'routine' is the most common solution to the problem. Menzies (1960) explained the splitting up of patient care into routine tasks in terms of it being a means of protecting the nurse from anxiety. This might be the real reason for the dislike of individualized care; the data allow no more than speculation.

The two extracts below describe management by 'routine', a style favoured by the students.

STUDENT: I've worked on a ward where the sister had quite definite ideas. I thought it was good. They also had written out, like a card, with what they called an oral hygiene round as well as a back round. The oral hygiene was done at 10 am, and after lunchtime, during the afternoon and after teatime and before they went to their beds at night; which I thought was very good and which I've never seen anywhere else (. . .). I thought it was good because it's something that's more or less forgotten about in a busy ward, you know the oral hygienes are never done two or four hourly, they are never done regularly, it's just when somebody has got nothing else to do that they seem to remember to do them, I found that it was very good (. . .).

KM: You think that by having a few set routines like that it does make sure that things get done rather than . . .

STUDENT: It sounds very laying down the rules, very military-like but I found that it worked well because things get done and you knew that things had been done, you know whereas you're starting something and somebody says 'oh, I've done that'. Nobody knows what

anybody else has done and half the time things either
get forgotten or they get done two and three times.

KM: How have you found the work organized on the ward,
          was it the same on all or different?

STUDENT: Well the first ward was really unorganized just
          running around all day trying to get through the
          work, getting shouted at for not doing this and not
          doing that. The second ward was very, very organized,
          you had this to do and then that to do another time,
          and you did get through the work, I think more
          efficiently.

KM: How was it organized, was it written down or . . .?

STUDENT: No, you were given a report in the morning and
          allocated to jobs and you had to do, say, all the charts,
          or you were caring for post-op patients.

KM: Which did you feel happier in?

STUDENT: Personally I felt happier in the ward where it was all in
          a muddle, because I like working where I've got
          something to do all the time and I can't say when I've
          finished this I just sit down.

KM: In the one that was in a muddle did you find that you
          had more variety of things to do?

STUDENT: Yes, on the other I was usually on charts, did dressings
          once. But on the first ward you did everything, I got an
          awful lot more experience.

The students appear to sympathize with the underlying principles
of patient allocation and tend to view this type of organization as
an 'in an ideal world' style. The fact of a ward full of patients makes
the operation of a system of individualized care seem, to the
students, almost impossible without resorting to routine blocks of
care to be 'got through' as a workload. As one student pointed out,
the seriously ill will be given individualized care anyway because
of the 'specialling' mode of care which co-exists in a system of
ward routines. Students' practical objections to patient allocation
were often rooted in their experience of 'specialling'. It is usually
the case that senior nurses 'special' patients and so when the idea of
patient allocation is considered, it is often rejected mostly on the
grounds that junior students would not be capable of taking care of
all the needs of one patient. The idea that less dependent patients

could be allocated to junior nurses seems to get lost in the debate.

Routinized care was favoured by some students because it represented a fool-proof system of getting through the work without items of care being missed out. Indeed it might be argued that the certainty which a routine provides would also benefit the patients. If an unfailing system of care is in operation, then the patient can rest assured that his needs will be met. Just as the students felt that with routines 'things get done', the patients might gain security from a similar belief. Routines, of course, are only as good as their makers and operators.

Management and non-management

So far, two styles of management have been described, one focusing on patients and the other on routines. Students were very much aware of the presence or absence of leadership on a ward. There were students, however, who described wards where the nursing work just seemed to happen. In other words, there was no overt management strategy coming from the ward sister. This non-management has implications for the organization of nursing work, in so far as it leaves room for alternative organizational forms to emerge. These alternative forms are discussed later in the chapter.

The notion of non-management emerged from students' comments about the type of ward organization which they enjoyed. The student who enjoyed the ward where 'it was all in a muddle' did so because she liked to be kept busy. She also got the opportunity to undertake a wider range of tasks than she would have managed on a ward which operated by routines.

This was not everyone's preference, however, as instanced in the following extract.

STUDENT: Well, I enjoy working in a ward where the person in charge knows what they are doing and knows what they want you to do. So you're told beforehand, you know, a certain job and I don't mind being given directions at all, because, well at my stage [first year] you can't, you're not in a position to organize yourself particularly well. So I like to know that the person in charge of the ward is, you know, has got it all thought out and I'm quite happy to, you know, get on with what I'm told to do (. . .).

KM: What is it about that, I mean you sound quite definite that you like it when the person at the top knows what they are doing. How does that affect your nursing?

STUDENT: Well you can concentrate on one particular job and you can get on with it and finish that and you know that you've got such and such to do. It, well gives you a more relaxed sort of attitude to working because if you are running about all over the place doing lots of little things and you're just about to do one thing and somebody comes up and says would you mind doing such and such, it throws me off balance. You know, you're rushing and probably not doing it properly (. . .). I think the sister's very important in that she can establish a good ward routine, which other people can, you know, carry on when she is not there.

KM: What sort of things go into a good routine would you say?

STUDENT: Well, it's sort of have certain things happen at certain times; like how much you actually achieve before you serve breakfast and you know whether patients should be bathed and things like that. So that you know, you can go on duty, you know exactly what's going to be happening in the morning and you can get on with it, and you're not sort of chopping and changing every-day but the sister knows things are happening in a logical sequence.

KM: So you know where you are.

STUDENT: Yes, you know how much more's to get done before lunch or tea.

Routine care then, can be seen in terms of tasks being performed by nurses in a timetabled order throughout the day. It is routine in the sense that it is a generalized approach to care rather than an individualized one. By thinking in terms of routines the care of the patients on a particular ward is seen in terms of 'nursing work' to be achieved by a certain time. Clearly, this state of affairs has differing consequences for patients, the students, the ward sister, and the permanent staff. The routine approach to care means that the ward sister can devise a timetable of tasks which can be handed out to student nurses according to their abilities. The students are, then, able to achieve the work by 'getting through' their allotted amount. The patients, it seems, do not necessarily receive many benefits from this system, except perhaps, that they can be sure of receiving their care. A benefit which should not be dismissed too lightly. There is a case to be made for the patient who is only interested in obtaining efficient nursing care; without any of the socio-psychological overlays which come with the individualized care ethic.

Strong (1979:223) has argued this point in the case of medicine.

'To understand medical service fully we must see it as just one of the many impersonal relationships into which consumers must enter in our society: doing the shopping, buying a house, selling a car, or seeing the doctor . . . what customers are most interested in is competent and efficient service, and they are quite prepared to sacrifice the more personal touches if this is the price they must pay. Few grocers have survived the super-market era.'

STUDENT: I think the patients must sort of feel that they are on an assembly line; first of all they get their beds made, then washed or bathed, oral hygiene. Don't all get everything done at once – there's no way you can do that – you can't go backwards and forwards, you would have everything out [i.e. the necessary equipment] (. . .).
KM: What do you think of that as a system?
STUDENT: It's OK for me, I don't know how the patient feels.

The idea that the ward is run to suit the needs of the staff rather than the patients was a recurrent one. One student pointed out that it was only as she got on in her training that she came to realize that the patients had to come first.

KM: Have you seen different wards organized in different ways, the ones you've worked in so far, have they got much in common or are they very different (. . .)? Is there anything you can carry from one ward to the next or are they . . .
STUDENT: No, there is an awful lot that you can carry on with you that you pick up. I think the main thing is that as you get on in your training you realize that your patient is the most important thing. I think with my first ward I tried to impress, not show off impress, but I tried to create a good impression and hopefully I

thought sister will think I'm a hard worker and I'm
caring. When we were busy I used to become harassed
if the patient was being slow and now I feel I'm totally
changed; sister can just wait, this patient is taking her
time, fair enough she's ill (. . .). A lot of basics you just
carry through, routines and everything.

KM: So how do wards differ from each other then? Do
different sisters have different ways of organizing
things?

STUDENT: Yes, some are a lot more trivial than others. In the
majority of wards you go and take a sphyg [momano-
meter] round and put thermometer in mouth, in one
ward you have to get a trolley for the case notes and
sphyg (. . .) and the sister goes mad if you don't do
that. Just these trivial things that annoy you that you
see no reason for and don't understand.

KM: How do you find out what to do, which trivial bits
suit?

STUDENT: Either a staff nurse or a student tells you or you get a
row from sister, it's as simple as that (. . .) you learn as
you go.

The student pointed out that many of the wards had much in
common, and that often the matters which present the students
with problems of adjustment as they move from ward to ward are
trivial. Her comments about putting the patient first, now that she
is a senior student, should perhaps be treated with caution. Whilst
she was not the only student to make this point, there is always the
possibility that such remarks are made in order to impress the
researcher. Taken at face value it seems that this student had
initially put the organization and ward routine first, not least
because she was attempting to impress the ward sister; only when
she became a more senior student did she put the patient first.

Official and unofficial ways of 'running the ward'

The provision of guidelines by the ward sister is not, of course, any
guarantee that they will be followed. One student said that 'a lot of
the good wards have care laid down . . . others the care given is
optional – so how good the care is depends on the student nurses on

the ward.' If a ward sister does not supervise and issue guidelines, the organization of care is determined by the students and staff. When this is the case the question of who does what may be settled according to the lines of the official hierarchy or the social structure of the ward. These structures are by no means independent of each other. Indeed, the interaction of the official hierarchy and the prevailing social structure on the ward is an important point to consider. The nursing hierarchy is a social reality with which the students must contend. Students, in negotiating their way through the ward, have to be aware of both the hierarchy and the informal social relationships which exist between members of the permanent staff.

The hierarchy which exists in the nursing structure is evident on many wards. This is relevant to the discussion in so far as the kinds of tasks carried out by the individual students on a ward, which does not have specific routines laid down by the ward sister, are often dictated both by their position in the hierarchy and their relationship with the permanent staff on that particular ward. The given hierarchy can be used as a dependable substitute for any more imaginitive division of labour which the ward sister might have devised. The use of the hierarchy, in terms of the who does what in the organization of ward nursing, was summed up neatly by one student who said: 'If you are a staff nurse you don't get a bedpan, if you are a third year you don't get a bedpan – if you've got no stripes [i.e. first-year student] you've got the bedpan!'

The ward sister is the person who sets the general tone of the ward and decides how the ward should be organized. At least, it is true to say that it is generally premised that the ward sister controls the ward. However, it is clear from these data that the way in which nursing care is actually organized at patient level does not always accord with the directives of the ward sister. This is the case because the ward sister is only one of the several people involved in the delivery of patient care. The ward sister operates according to her own ideas about running a ward, yet she does this in the context of a nursing hierarchy, from auxiliaries, to students to staff nurses. The students are, generally speaking, willing to please and are used to obeying ward sisters' instructions; however, the trained staff and auxiliaries are in a different position with respect to the sister and as such form a social substructure with which the student must contend. So although the ward sister is ostensibly the person who dictates how the patient care shall be given, the forces in operation beneath her can have a profound effect upon how the ward actually works. This is equally true of wards where the sister manages, and does not manage the nurses.

There seem to be several options, not necessarily mutually exclusive, pertaining to how the ward was 'run'. The sister as official leader could adopt a firm role and control the nursing work either by patient-centred or routine task-centred methods. In either case the sister has to have some means of exposing her style to the staff and students so that they know what is expected of them. The management style can be revealed in various ways, from the very overt tactics of work books, closely prescribed, supervised and accounted-for care running either along individualized or routine lines, to a total lack of direction from the sister, in which case other mechanisms came into operation.

Students gave accounts of both task-centred and patient-centred organization of nursing work. Some students expressed a preference for patient-centred nursing, but readily accepted the necessity for a routinized approach because this was a safe way of getting work done. Knowing what to do and being occupied were central concerns for the student nurse, and active management by the ward sister, on the whole, met both of these needs. If direct supervision was not given by the sister there were two major alternatives. Either the official organizational hierarchy comes into play when the staff nurses, enrolled nurses, and senior students more or less decide what will happen or the informal social structure is used to bring some order to the work. This informal subculture, which can develop quite strongly on a ward or among a group of students, then becomes the major organizational force which ensures that the patients are cared for.

We will now examine the effect of the official hierarchical structure and the informal social structure. The typical situation in which subculture rule emerges was described by one student who said:

'Obviously people's ability to organize varies a lot – some wards are very well run, you know exactly where you are; at report each person is told who to work with and what to do (. . .). On other wards everyone scatters after the report and does their own thing.'

Such a 'scattering' with no directives from the ward sister leaves the path open for some other means of running the ward coming into effect. Several students mentioned that if they worked on a disorganized ward the students often got together and organized themselves. This type of student co-operation is all the more effective if the students are from the same set[1] or are friends outside the hospitals, as was sometimes the case. This subculture approach to organizing patient care is dependent upon the hierarchical nature of the official organizational structure of the ward or the co-existent social structure. The importance of the social structure was highlighted by one student who said right at the start of the interview that she always likes to know who she is working with for the shift.

The permanent staff of a ward, that is the trained staff and the auxiliaries, often formed a social group of their own and ran the ward on the basis of this informal structure. A common complaint among the student nurses was that trained staff, especially staff nurses, often left the students to do the work whilst they enjoyed prolonged coffee breaks in the office. It was during the discussions of ward organization that the question arose of whether the ward sister or staff nurses when they are in charge should join in as part of the workforce on the ward.

KM: Have you got any preference for the way some of the
           ward sisters have organized the way the actual nursing
           is carried out, who does what etc.?
STUDENT: Not really. I like when the staff nurse helps in a ward
           and the ward sister helps as well. You find in a lot of
           wards the staff nurses go and drink coffee and things
           like that, if the ward isn't that busy and the students are
           left to get on with all the boring tasks, like a care
           round.[2] I think with a care round, well it's up to the
           whole ward team to try and help, because it can be so
           heavy and takes so long. When it comes to charts and
           things I think the staff nurses should help as well,
           because you find in casualty and theatre staff nurses are
           great at helping; it's them in charge. In wards you

[1] 'Set' refers to the group of students who begin their training together.

[2] Where all the patients are offered some form of a 'wash and brush up'. It may also involve pressure area care.

sometimes find it's the senior student in charge because the staff nurse is always in her room; she may have the doctors, the report, and a lot of paperwork, but I still feel that in a lot of cases they could try and come into the ward and mix with the patients, if not with the staff.

The fact that the work is 'heavy' was often the main reason put forward by the students for wanting the trained staff to join in and help out. This is consistent with the students' notion of there being a job to be done and with their desire for an 'all hands on deck' approach to doing it. Leaving aside what they would have liked to do, the main aims of the nurses, in particular on the long stay wards, centred around getting through the work (work being defined in terms of physical tasks). The language they used to describe the work emphasized this: 'the work load'; 'working hard'; 'pulling your weight'; 'pulling together'; 'mucking in'.

The student quoted above referred to the tasks which the students were left to do as 'boring tasks' and cited the care round as an example. It is interesting to note that the particular task that she dismissed as 'boring', is one of the number of nursing activities which can be said to be independent of medical orders. Ironically whilst there is a move to increase independent nursing activity and develop a 'body of nursing knowledge' to this end, it is this very practice which is regarded as boring and best left to the students.

Braverman's (1974) notion of degraded work is relevant here. The work is split into a number of steps in the labour process, these steps are divorced from knowledge so that the work can be carried out by less qualified personnel. The staff nurses and sisters could be said to be adopting the role of overseers with the necessary knowledge for planning and ordering care, with the students as the deskilled workforce. The students estimate behaviour of the trained staff on the basis of how much of the 'boring' work they shirk. Boring tasks, incidentally, do not require any particular knowledge for their performance, as evidenced by the fact that they can be carried out equally well by students and auxiliaries.

Routines

Students considered that routines are, to an extent, inevitable if care is to be rendered by institutions. Patients are categorized according to medical condition and care is dealt out in routinized batches by both medical staff and, following their example, by the nursing staff. By the nature of things, many of the needs of patients are held in common, the normal functions which they generally perform for themselves according to what might even be considered to be a fairly common timetable must be met by the institution. Thus, eating, washing, and sleeping times are scheduled according to the hospital's idea of an average day. Routines are problematic on two main counts. Firstly, they may very readily get out of step with their purpose and thus begin to meet ends other than those for which they were primarily designed. Secondly, routines are to an extent all-absorbing. If some matters can be dealt with routinely, why not others? Routine then becomes the only line of approach to any task or situation. In the latter case, routines can become petty and irritating, seemingly serving no purpose other than the proliferation of routine. This is a particular problem with hospital or ward routines.

Ward routines can be described in terms of external and internal routines; the former are those which are imposed on the ward from the wider hospital context, examples would be meal times, visiting hours, doctor's rounds. The distinction, it must be remembered, is an analytic not an empirical one. It merely serves to clarify a discussion of the data. Internal routines are those which are specific to and within the control of the ward, such things as when patients are bathed, ward reports given, etc. Axiomatically the external routines put constraints on the organization of each individual ward and thus dictate, or at least limit the scope of internal routines. External routines, once grasped by students, can be transferred from ward to ward, whereas internal ones must be learnt afresh each time. All wards are in some senses similar to each other and in others they are different: it is the external routines which make them similar and the internal ones which make them different.

The notion of 'getting through the work' was frequently linked to the idea of ward routine. The idea of a certain amount of work to be got through before a certain time was common. If nursing is conceived of in these terms it rapidly becomes an activity divorced from the care of patients. Routine is to some extent reified and self-serving. 'Running the ward' takes on its own character and although in the first instance strategies for organizing patient care *en masse* were developed of necessity, there is a tendency for the machinery of organization to take over. The essential nature of nursing can be sacrificed to the organization of care, which is indeed ironic as the patient, the object of the care, is the *raison d'être* for the organization itself.

Getting through the work in this routinized way appealed to those among the students who enjoyed the fast pace of the work. Some of the students expressed a liking for 'being busy' as distinct from 'looking busy'. This is illustrated in the extract below. Surgical wards were often preferred to medical wards on the grounds that they were more exciting, had a faster patient turnover, and ran at a quicker pace.

KM: One of the things that keeps cropping up in these interviews is people talking about 'running the ward' and 'getting the work done', like you said a list of tasks to be done, it never seems to bear much resemblance to the total patient care bit, that you get in college. Do you find a big difference?

STUDENT: Oh yes, college is obviously to the book – you go to the ward and everybody does their own thing. I find that as well, as long as you get through the work, it doesn't matter about the patient, you've done your work. (. . .) If you sat down and talked to patients which is what they need up there, even as a junior nurse you can talk. They [the staff] get really mad, you should be working sort of thing. But you are there to talk to the patient as well (. . .).

KM: Even there that wasn't seen as doing something. You have touched on something else which crops up – this constant looking busy, even if there is nothing to do.

STUDENT: Mm mmm.

KM: Where does that feeling come from, does anyone actually tell you that you must always do something?

STUDENT: No, it's just they look at you 'now what are you doing nurse just standing there you should be rushing and looking as if you're working'. It's always the impression you get. I've never been anywhere where they allow you to stand around if there is nothing to do; you have got to do something.

It is interesting to note how this student makes the distinction between doing the work and looking after the patient. She also points out the need to be seen to be busy, which many of the students discussed. Again, this is consistent with Clarke's findings:

> 'Talking or listening or waiting for a patient to do something for herself, are regarded as less work-like than "doing" something for the patient such as dressing or bathing. Some of the patients shared this view, "you'll catch it, haven't you anything else to do?", they joked with nurses who sat down and talked for any length of time.'
>
> (Clarke 1978:79)

The notions of being busy and getting through the work seem to be tied to the question of for whose benefit is the ward being 'run'. Routines are tied to the shift system of hospital nursing and the amount of work to be done through the routines was often timetabled according to the hospital shifts. The division between night and day staff is well recognized in nursing. The students referred to the clash of routines between shifts which often run independently of each other. An example was given of back rounds, or oral hygiene rounds being carried out in quick succession, that is at 8.30 pm by the day staff and repeated at 9.30 pm by the night staff. Similar clashes were described in the mornings.

The overriding concern of each shift seemed to have to do with getting through the work which was considered to be the province of one shift before the next shift arrived on duty. Even when unexpected setbacks occurred which put the routine behind schedule, the most important goal was still to accomplish that shift's work on time.

Much of the rush and adherence to routine could be attributed to the general uncertainty of ward life. If there is at least one thing which can be relied upon, namely the routine, other calamities can be coped with in some way. This uncertainty factor is a fairly sound justification for the hurried nature of nursing work if it is considered within the context of individual shifts, and this, according to the students, does appear to be the way in which the work is conceived and divided up. The nurses are continually working quickly in case the unexpected crops up and throws the schedule out of phase. The rush, after a crisis, which is necessary to remain on schedule, is anticipated and employed before any crisis occurs in a 'just in case' sense. Thus, nursing care is carried out in a series of hurried routines with a sense of only just keeping ahead of time in case some delaying event should arise. Clearly, if there were not seen to be such rigid divisions between what work is appropriate to one shift to do as opposed to the next, this rushed approach to nursing would be redundant. The routine would then cease to be the driving force, instead it could become an organizational tactic for ensuring that nursing care was given in an unhurried manner.

Professional judgement – following routines

The debate about the overall desirability of routine versus individualized approaches to patient care has implications beyond the simple question: Does the patient receive his care? It raised issues of delegation and accountability, professionalism in nursing, and the place of professionals or future professionals (the students) in the context of an organization. I have already suggested that routinized, carefully prescribed care can, to a large extent, obviate any need for the exercise of professional judgement on the part of the nurse. If the nursing work is organized along individualized care lines, then the questions of the use of professional judgment and discretion on the part of the nurse are more likely to arise. In concrete terms, in the routine-style organizational setting the nursing work could be labelled 'charts, dressings, and water jugs' for one nurse; and 'bed baths, oral care' for another. In the individualized care system, nurses are allocated a group of patients. Clearly, if the work is allocated in this way the room for the use of discretion on the part of the student is greater in the latter case. Although it should be remembered that the care plan for individual patients might well spell out the care in some detail and thus decrease the discretionary potential for the student nurse.

The students appear to require a certain amount of independence in their work, yet they need to be sure about what is expected of them in order to exercise this discretion. Discretion, however, has to be considered against the overall pattern of ward organization and the nursing hierarchy. Discretionary limits can be set to student work, whether they are involved in a system of individualized care or task-oriented routinized care. The question of direction and supervision proved to be a moot point among the students. Broadly, it could be said that the more senior students began to resent supervision as they became experienced, whereas the junior nurses appreciated it. This indeed was not a surprising discovery. The consequences of the presence or absence of ward sisters' dictates are, however, of interest. If students are to become qualified practising nurses in their own right, they do need supervision in order to attain this status. By the same token, if care on the ward is to be organized as a communal activity, trained staff and learners alike must follow the directives of one overall controller, namely, the ward sister. However, it must be said that with the shorter working week the ward sister is absent from the ward for a large proportion of the time. Difficulties arise if the trained staff wish to exercise professional autonomy and make their own clinical decisions on the basis of professional judgement, and if the senior students wish to flex their muscles in this same direction. Clearly, the students are more easily contained because as learners they do not have the authority upon which to act independently. It does, however, raise interesting questions about the organization of the training of nurses, and the exercise of the professional judgement to which, as registered nurses, they must lay claim.

The ward sister is faced with patients to care for and an unqualified workforce with which to effect the care. The question of the supervision of the students' work is therefore crucial. It seems that there are at least two alternative types of solution to the problem of supervision, namely, *bureaucratic* and *professional*. The ward sister may well feel justified in resorting to the tactic of degradation of the work; that is to say divorcing it as far as possible from specialist knowledge and reducing it to simple labour (Braverman 1974), in order that the students might carry it out. In so far as the students saw themselves to be interchangeable with the auxiliaries in the workforce, this tactic has a degree of plausibility. That is, until we consider that the student nurses are moving towards a position when they too will be qualified and, if the professional model is accepted, they should carry out their nursing work on the basis of their knowledge and professional judgement. The difficulty with this lies in the fact that the students have had no experience during their training of exercising professional judgement.

It could be argued that the ward sister's recourse to this division of labour approach to achieving nursing care stems from the fact that she has always nursed in terms of groups of tasks, rather than on the basis of any professional judgement, and so still plans care along the same lines. In other words, it is unrealistic to suppose that the student is progressing towards attaining a position from which she will nurse according to a *professional* judgement model. The ward sister may simply not have moved on from the conceptualization of nursing organization that she employed in her own student days, consequently she organizes care bureaucratically. The bureaucratic approach need not, then, be a conscious intellectual decision, rather a matter of applying what the sister learned as a student. The bureaucratic system involves dividing the patients up into entities of care which are graded and carried out by students of appropriate seniority, or indeed by auxiliaries of sufficient long-standing.

Professionals in organizations

The discussion in this chapter lays much of the groundwork for a consideration of nursing in relation to the notion of profession. So far, the main argument has been that nursing is conceived of as work to be got through by a workforce of student nurses and auxiliaries, whilst the qualified 'professionals' look on from their position as managers. However, as it has been suggested earlier, there are difficulties involved in accepting the *professional* model, because nursing takes place within the hospital organization. The co-existence of a bureaucratic hierarchical management system in nursing and the fact that several qualified nurses may work together at the same time in the same ward creates a contradiction which must be resolved. One option might be that individual staff nurses are given both authority and the attendant accountability for the care of a number of patients. In this way each qualified nurse can exercise her own professional judgment and work accordingly. The evidence of this study suggests that this style of management is rarely encountered, although it is beyond the scope of this work to say more than that. The questions of professionalizing and professionalism are addressed later, for the present we shall simply introduce the problematic issue of professionals working within organizations which are run along bureaucratic lines.

Stinchcombe (1959) in a study of construction work, argued that

'the greater degree of professionalisation of its labour force enables the construction industry to function with a minimum

i

of bureaucratisation. The workers employed are for the most part skilled craftsmen who can perform their tasks without much direction and control from superiors because their work is guided by standards of craftsmanship which are akin to professional standards. In short, a professionalised labour force constitutes an alternative to the bureaucratic organisation of work.'

(reported in Blau and Scott 1963:208)

If we accept for a moment that nursing is a profession, then Stinchcombe's remarks have some relevance for nursing. Also, nursing carried out along 'standards of craftsmanship' lines, or even *professional* lines, could provide a more sanguine outlook for the student nurse. If 'craftsmen' are to be found in the wards, then the student may well be apprenticed to them in a rather more satisfactory way than the present data of this study suggest.

3

LEARNING AND WORKING

So far we have seen how the students go about presenting themselves as part of the nursing workforce, and how they fit into the organizational structure of the hospital wards. At this point it is perhaps worth reminding ourselves that these students are still in the process of becoming nurses and are as much a part of the college of nursing as they are of the wards. In this chapter we shall see how the students manage to straddle the college/ward divide, and how they cope with doing the work of nurses. These issues raise some fundamental questions about what level of theoretical[1] input a registered nurse requires in the basic training programme.

The students saw the college as a source of the theoretical input to their training and the place where they learned the correct way to carry out practical nursing. On the wards, however, they found that not only were college techniques not used, but that nursing auxiliaries often had as much, if not more, responsibility as the students for the basic care of patients. The students' accounts of the college versus ward divide led to a discussion of the place of 'theory' in nursing and a questioning of whether it was, in fact, necessary. That is to say, if the students and auxiliaries functioned in a similar way, what was the justification for the theoretical component of nursing education? The competence of the student as a worker, capable of undertaking the necessary tasks to complete the nursing care routines, is examined in the context of her supposed student role; thus, the *service* versus *education* division is explored. This discussion has implications for the needs of student nurses throughout their training in terms of support and guidance.

---

[1] 'Theoretical' is used here in the way that the students use the term, that is to describe the content of their lectures.

College versus ward

One of the most notable features of the students' account of their nursing world was the gap between nursing as taught in the college of nursing and nursing as it was experienced on the wards. This fact of student nurse life is not in any way new. Indeed it is almost a part of the nursing folklore that these differences exist. Olesen and Whittaker (1968:143) found that student nurses in their study experienced the same phenomenon:

> 'Perhaps the most exquisite dilemma of all with respect to faculty–staff relationships lay in instruction. It was incumbent on faculty to indicate what they thought were the best ways of doing things, ways that sometimes ran counter to what students saw staff doing on the wards.'

What is particularly interesting is the fact that, whilst the differences are profound, the students accepted them quite readily. It was generally held that the college should teach the 'correct' way to do things, but in the real world, because of a shortage of time, the 'correct' way is modified to suit the prevailing situation on the wards. At the operational level, this ward/college difference is a clear cut fact of the student nurses' life. Student nurses are taken into the health service on what is essentially an apprenticeship basis. Their time is divided between lectures and demonstrations in the college of nursing and practical experience on the wards, in a variety of specialties. The students form a large part of the workforce in hospital wards. Although they always work under supervision, as they are not legally qualified to practise independently, the degree of supervision varies enormously. One of the major difficulties facing these student nurses, it seemed, was balancing the roles of worker and learner. The dichotomy is becoming ever more apparent as the colleges of nursing move in the direction, albeit slowly, of other institutions of higher education. That is to say, the student nurse is being encouraged to develop the student side of the role, and this throws the worker element into greater relief. The students naturally learn much of their practical nursing skill in the hospital wards, and so they have to determine how to select the 'good' from the 'bad' influences which they encounter. They must then develop a style of work, with both the qualified staff and the auxiliaries, which will allow them to function in the wards in such a way as to facilitate their learning. This facilitation is achieved in part by the way they relate to the permanent staff, but largely by their willingness and ability to be a member of the workforce on the ward.

The students are aware of the differences between the college ways of 'doing nursing' and those of the permanent staff of the wards. Since the student nurse spends much of her time on the wards it is at one level a matter of simple expediency which leads her to perfect ways of discovering and complying with the 'ward ways' of nursing.

KM: How much do you think what you are taught in the college affects how you nurse, rather than what you see people do in the wards?

STUDENT: I think it is, you know, you get taught in the school the proper way for everything, but you've never got time to do the proper way in the wards (. . .). The theory is good, you need it, what you get, but like the nursing they just sort of teach you the basics in the school and the proper way to do it so that when you go into the wards, I mean, you've got, well you know what should be done, what's going on so that you're not really totally ignorant about what's getting done (. . .).

This student had no difficulty in both seeing and accepting the fact that the style of nursing taught in the college did not resemble exactly that found in the wards. Although she recognizes that the college teaches the 'proper' way of nursing, her later comment about knowing 'what's going on' when she is on the ward indicates an important function of the college. This has to do with introducing the students to sufficient theory to allow them to function as part of the ward staff. Clearly, if a student nurse was entirely unaware of the possible range of events which might surround different categories of patients, she would not make a useful member of the ward staff. Thus, although there is not deemed to be time on the ward for nurses to carry out procedures in the 'college way', the college teaching seems to furnish the background information which enables students to function on the wards.

Another student said that she preferred an orderly ward where things were done 'properly', this led to a discussion of where she learned to nurse 'properly'.

KM: . . . and you find the way the sister organizes the work affects the way you actually nurse?

STUDENT: Yes, because if you've got somebody who is really slightly slapdash – the permanent members of staff tend to be like that you know. They say 'don't bother doing it like that' [in the case of some dressings being done in the bathroom]; it's not sterile at all and you feel, well this isn't really right, but when somebody says, 'we haven't really time to do that, just stick a bit of gauze on', that's it. I feel that if the sister were here (. . .).

KM: How does that affect you and your development as a nurse?

STUDENT: Well it worries me from time to time, because I like it when I go to a ward where things are done properly, you know, things are done the right way. And I think at the same time it also makes you awfully, well you change, you go to another ward and do things as you have been doing them in the other place (. . .).

KM: When you relate back to the proper way of doing it, where do you pick that up from, do you know?

STUDENT: (. . .) Well, I think in the school you are taught the correct way of doing it but you have to make slight modification when working in the ward or you can still manage to do things properly.

This student started out by giving an example of how things were not always done 'properly' on the ward. By the end of the exchange she was saying that the differences were really mere modifications of the 'proper way'. She did not attribute any blame to the trained staff who were doing the 'sterile' dressing in the bathroom but thought that if the ward sister were present things would be done 'properly'.

Breaking the rules

The students appeared to sanction the 'ward way' of doing things because it was efficient and worked, even though it was not entirely correct. There are studies in industrial sociology which illustrate similar behaviour in organizations. On the one hand, there are hard and fast rules which must be seen to be obeyed and not dismissed as impractical; and on the other, these same rules are frequently broken. The breaking of the rules is a necessary part of the smooth functioning of the organization; new members must be taught that this is, in an informal sense, a legitimate activity. Bensman and Gerver (1963) describe the breaking of one rule in an airplane factory in the United States. The use of the 'tap' is a means of achieving alignments in assembling aircraft wings, where during the production process the correct alignment between nuts and plate openings have become distorted. Use of the 'tap' is both dangerous and forbidden, yet it is frequently used with the unofficial sanction of the foremen. Bensman and Gerver argue that analysis of deviancy within an organization using a functionalist approach is not helpful. This, they say, is because it assumes a total approach; all parts of the organization working towards the same ends. In such an analytic approach deviation from the rules implies a rejection of the norms of the system; the authors suggest a different analytic approach, which says people, not systems, have ends and that these are accommodated in collective behaviour. They found that from the viewpoint of production the use of the 'tap' is imperative to the smooth functioning of the production organization, even though it is one of the most serious work crimes. This is recognized even at official levels.

The students in this study described behaviour which they knew to be incorrect, yet could also justify in the name of accomplishing the task in hand. The student's comment about such behaviour not happening when the ward sister was there illustrates the fact that some notion of right and wrong was operating. One could speculate that the sisters knew very well what was going on, but unofficially chose to ignore it.

Similar deviant, yet accepted and organizationally necessary, behaviour was described by Ditton (1977) in the case of bread salesmen. This involved 'fiddling the customer' and Ditton explains how new workers were socialized into this behaviour: 'institutionalised socialising arguments are deliberately constructed by the bakery management to teach recruits to regularly and invisibly rob customers on behalf of the company.'

Whilst it is not being suggested that similar criminal behaviour goes on in hospital, the industrial analogy is interesting. It seems that the acceptance of an 'official' set of rules alongside organizationally acceptable deviance is not peculiar to nursing. This acceptance is evidenced in the comments of another student who thought that the nursing practised on the wards was not too different from school: 'the big difference is that the corners are cut, in school you do the whole thing, on the wards sometimes you don't have the time.'

The overriding impression given by the students in their discussion of the differences between the wards and the college was that of a matter of fact approach to the divide. Although they came to study nursing at the college of nursing, it seemed that the student nurses were not in the least perturbed by the discrepancies between college and ward nursing.

The clinical teacher

The differences between the wards and the college of nursing is perhaps best highlighted in the consideration of the function of the clinical teacher. The clinical teacher is a member of the staff of the college, but is responsible for the practical side of the teaching, and thus most of the clinical teaching takes place on the wards.

KM: Is there much relationship between what is taught in the college and what you see on the wards?

STUDENT: No, you have not got time to do what they tell you. Some of the things, like say in some wards, they go just about right by the book, but in other wards it's just a case of do what you can by the book. Carry on as best you can. It is just using your common sense.

KM: I just wondered, you hear people talking about running the ward as if it is something different from anything else that goes on . . .

STUDENT: I think a lot of teachers in the school should go back into the wards for a while, because, I mean, you get teachers telling you things and you go into the wards and you just cannot relate anything to what they have said at all (. . .). They do go around the wards, but I do not think they are there long enough to see what actually goes on; and then everybody is on their best behaviour.

The student went on to say how working with a clinical teacher on the wards was not similar to the way ward work was usually carried out:

STUDENT: (. . .) in the school you would be there for hours if you were doing a bed bath, I mean, say if you were on the surgical ward and you have got 25 patients, you cannot take an hour on each patient or you would be there for the rest of your life.

KM: And when your tutors and clinical teachers come into the ward do they actually work with you? Obviously they do not do everything at the speed you would do without them; do they just take you and one patient and pretend it is like it was in school?

STUDENT: Huh, huh, that is exactly how they do it. It is just one patient and everybody else is wiped off the map.

It seems that the ward/college divide does not exist on all wards to the same extent. The relationship between the clinical teacher and the ward staff varies. In some cases the ward sister and the clinical teacher strike up a good working relationship and so the resultant experience can be a realistic one for the student. On the other hand, as the last student's comments demonstrate, the clinical teacher can be seen as the college brought to the ward and whenever she chooses to work with a student for a few hours, the student is judged to be a pair of hands lost to the ward. Although the reality is that the clinical teacher represents an extra pair of hands; the fact that she wishes to nurse according to the ways of the college, rather than the faster adapted ward ways, negates her contribution to the workforce.

The clinical teachers were seen to belong to the college of nursing, yet at times they furthered the service ends of the ward rather than the educational needs of the students. Clinical teachers were also seen by some students to be closer in touch with the reality of the ward situation than were their colleagues in the college; they could help the students to adapt their college training to the ward requirements. One student gave a rather extreme example of this when she described her experiences as a first year student on a gynaecological ward. She had been told in the college that junior students would not be required to collect major surgical patients from theatre; they might conceivably be required to bring patients back after minor operations. The clinical teacher had shown her what to do in both circumstances 'just in case'. This precautionary measure was taken by the clinical teacher because the ward had no allocation of senior students; thus, the chances of a first year student nurse having to undertake a senior student's duties were high. The clinical teacher anticipated service needs and allowed these to subordinate the student's educational needs by introducing, out of context, the necessary knowledge for the care and transport of major surgical patients. This 'crash course' approach was dictated by the needs of the ward not those of the student.

A similar happening was sometimes described in relation to night duty. One student described her experience as a junior night nurse saying 'you are not supposed to be in charge as a junior on nights, but I was because we were short staffed'. She enjoyed this experience and said that she gained confidence through it. It was the return to day duty which presented problems; when, she said, 'everything is taken away from you, and you're back to just being a wee student who doesn't really know very much.' In this case the extra responsibility was seen by the student to be a positive learning experience; yet, in service terms, it was clearly just an expedient measure. The withdrawal of responsibility once experienced, was frustrating for the student. In some senses this oscillation of responsibility, depending upon the prevailing circumstances, is one of the underlying difficulties for the student throughout training. It is a theme to which I will return in the following discussion of student and nursing auxiliary relations.

Students and auxiliaries

In the light of these examples, it seems that the student nurses are trying to do two things during their three years of training. The first is the *raison d'être* of their presence in the health service, namely to gain registration. The second is to function efficiently as a member of the main workforce of nursing. These two aspects of the student nurse's activity are never mutually exclusive by virtue of the fact that in order to obtain registration the student must put in a given number of hours of practical nursing in a series of prescribed areas. This practical experience must be accomplished satisfactorily, according to the standards of the ward staff. In order to meet these standards, it appears that the students must display an ability to function as part of the workforce of the ward. However, there remains the important question of emphasis – whether service or educational needs are given priority.

The students spoke a great deal about the amount of responsibility which they had on the wards; this was often discussed in relation to the work that the nursing auxiliaries did and the students' position, in terms of authority, *vis-a-vis* the auxiliaries. There were mixed feelings among the students towards the auxiliaries, largely because of the tension which exists between their reliance on the auxiliary for help in getting to know the ward routines and their insistence upon some differentiation between auxiliary work and nursing work.

Students sometimes felt that, as junior nurses, they had often been passed over for a nursing auxiliary if there was a job to be done which the sister or staff nurse knew the auxiliary would be able to do more quickly. It takes more time to explain and show something to a student than it does to ask another, already competent, person to do the job. Nevertheless, the students saw the value of the auxiliaries and were quick to defend them if they thought that I was being in any way critical of them. On one such occasion I had suggested that the students had some basis, other than experience, upon which to make their decisions and so, even though on the face of it the auxiliary nurse appeared to be more competent, the student had a more legitimate stance from which to proceed, namely the 'theoretical' component of their training. The student responded by saying that 'lots of auxiliary nurses were very good', and that a lot depended upon the personality of both the nurse and auxiliary. I pursued the point about nurses working from a knowledge base whereas the auxiliaries depended upon past experience, which it has to be said was sometimes considerable. This met with a firm defence of auxiliary nurses.

One student's comment exemplifies the students' feeling that the ward sisters tended to go to the auxiliaries before the students when they wanted work done.

KM: Do you ever find that auxiliaries are doing the things that students should be doing, because they have this relationship with the ward sister?

STUDENT: Yes, it's not supposed to happen, as far as the nursing officers are concerned it doesn't happen; but it does, a lot. They take the upper hand, especially with the junior nurses.

KM: Is that hospital-wide or particular wards?

STUDENT: Particular wards. I think on the surgical side they tend more, the auxiliaries do their own work; bed baths –

              things like that, they tend to do their own work, water jugs and things. On the medical side they tend to do nurses' work, things students could be doing.

KM: What sort of things on the medical wards?

STUDENT: Things like, they'll tell the student what they should do with this patient; you know like 'this is how we get them up' – like one the other day, a patient had to get a bandage taken off and have his foot re-bandaged, she just took it off and bandaged it up.

Another student, when talking about geriatric nursing, said that there was no difference in the work of students and auxiliaries; even in those areas of care where some technical nursing knowledge is required.

STUDENT: (. . .) I think there is nothing wrong with auxiliaries except when something technical does come along they think that because they have been there for years they have the expertise and start telling you what to do 'you shouldn't be doing that like that nurse', that sort of thing. It gets you quite annoyed because you think, I know that you have been here for years but you haven't done any theoretical side of it and you don't really know what you are doing, just because you've seen other people doing it.

KM: So really I think that is what I was getting at, I'm not actually suggesting that we should do away with nurse training. But you are there as the workforce, but quite often you are not allowed to put your thinking into practice, because you have got to do whatever is done there. It seems to be what people are saying in these interviews, what would you say about that?

STUDENT: I would agree with that. Most places have a set routine. I suppose they have to but you've got to stick to it and if you have any ideas you get 'we don't do that here dearie, get on with it'.

The observations of the first student are of interest because they serve to highlight the areas of nursing which she was to prepared to recognize and defend as 'nursing'. She resented the interference of the auxiliary nurse in overtly technical tasks, such as sterile dressings and bandaging; while she was not prepared to distinguish between her own *basic* care of a patient and that offered by an auxiliary. This view she maintained, even when in the interview I pointed out, at some length, that the auxiliary can only, for example, look after stroke patients so long as each patient behaves in much the same way as the last. That is to say, the auxiliary can only work from past experience, whereas the nurse's theoretical background, which naturally benefits from experience, enables her to plan care, and anticipate reactions without previous personal experience of the situation. The common sense knowledge which the auxiliaries exhibit should not be underestimated. My comments, made in order to see what the student would say about the difference between her and the auxiliaries, were perhaps a little too polarized. The auxiliary as a functioning front line worker cannot be considered to be devoid of a store of experience which has been assimilated into some working knowledge at a common sense level. However, the second student recognized the distinction between knowledge and experience as a basis for nursing action.

The nursing auxiliary is, for the student, an important force to be reckoned with. When the students arrive on a ward they need the auxiliary, for it is the auxiliary who, more often than not, initiates them. When the students eventually find their feet, they seem to have difficulty in shaking off their previous dependence upon the auxiliary, who remains an important figure and not one to be criticized or belittled. The logical conclusion to this kind of argument is that in practice there is, in some areas, very little difference between the work of the student nurse and that of the auxiliary. On the surgical wards there is possibly more of a distinction because of the amount of technical work to be done.

The work of the auxiliary, as portrayed by the students, is of some importance, particularly when the auxiliary is a long-standing member of the ward team. The auxiliary is in a potentially powerful position, even though she is at the bottom of the hierarchy; the students rely upon her for guidance in their early days on a ward and the ward sisters make extensive use of them. Mechanic's (1968:416) discussion of the power sources of the 'lower participants' in complex organizations is relevant here. 'It is not unusual for lower participants in complex organisations to assume and wield power and influence not associated with their formally defined positions within these organisations.'

Mechanic argues that these workers have personal power and no authority. There is a distinction to be made, he says, between formal and informal power. The formal power holders in an organization are those near the top of the hierarchy, by virtue of their formally structured access to information and personnel. Yet, Mechanic says: 'lower participants in organisations are frequently successful in manipulating the formal structure because they may have informally attained control over access to information, persons, and instrumentalities' (Mechanic 1968: 418). This type of informal power, he suggests, is often gained where there are 'numbers of well entrenched lower-ranking employees, and at the same time high rates of turnover among higher-ranking persons in the organisation'. This, of course, sums up the position of auxiliaries and student nurses in hospital wards.

'Practice' versus 'theory'

This line of discussion led to an exploration of the place of theory in nursing. 'Theory' is the term which the students used to describe their college lectures, in other words the bookwork, as opposed to their practical work. Thus, 'theory' does not have anything to do with 'theories of nursing' – it is simply the term used by the students in contradistinction to 'practice'. If nursing auxiliaries, who receive little or no training, can do most of the nursing which takes place, why have a large theoretical input in the general nurse training?

During discussion with one student the question of practical versus theoretical nursing arose. Whilst most students would, with varying degrees of conviction, defend the need for 'theory' in nurse training, this student thought it was not all that important.

KM: What I'm really interested in is what you think about nursing, if it helps, to start with patient care.

STUDENT: The comfort of the patient is really important as well . . .

KM: How do you . . .

STUDENT: Your attitude towards the patient physically and mentally, you know, telling the patient; how gentle you are with the patient. The practical side of nursing I think is more important than the theoretical side at the moment, as a student nurse, the responsibilities you are given as a student nurse, makes it more important to be more practical than theoretical, I think.

KM: (. . .) What would you call theoretical, do you see it as two separate sides of the . . .

STUDENT: It's not always two separate sides, eventually things throughout your training do click together better; but as far as practical nursing, when you're with the patients on the ward just doing your basic nursing care without thinking what's actually wrong with the patient, as with the 'nursing process', you work from the 'nursing care plan' without really knowing the diagnosis or what's wrong with the patient.

Another student defended the place of theory because she thought that it was intrinsically interesting.

KM: Do you find that you learn more on the wards or in the college, or is it different things that you learn?

STUDENT: You learn more on the wards but you learn while you are doing them (. . .), you sort of say this is done for such and such a reason, but in college you've got it down on paper, you've got it in your books exactly why it's done. The practical you learn on the wards, but it's best to know the theory behind it.

KM: Yes, because from some of the conversations I've had it almost seems that there are two things going on – you are learning all the things that you need to write down to pass the exam on the one hand, and then things are so different, in some ways, on the ward and other things you don't really have to know so long as you do the work.

STUDENT: I like to know why I'm doing things. I'm curious – at school I found subjects that I had to understand easier than the ones you just learnt off a page, because I like to know why I do things. That is what I've found in this block actually [the student was in the college for a 'study block' at the time of the interview], quite difficult because you had doctors' lectures and the exams weren't on the doctors' lectures; your exams were on the nursing care, and I was getting so caught up with all the little blood cells moving around

KM: [reference to haematology lectures]. Then I was thinking but I don't need to know that, but then it was nice to know that in the background.

KM: Is there a tendency to feel that the learning theory side of it is condition, signs, symptoms, and biology or what have you, and that really the nursing does not figure very largely, or does it, in what you feel you have to learn?

STUDENT: I don't really think it figures very large at all. I mean it's nice to know but when you are actually nursing in the ward (. . .) because you are doing the procedure you're not really thinking I am doing this because of such and such a reason (. . .).

When the students discussed practical as opposed to theoretical nursing, they were not always referring to the same phenomenon. The student just cited clearly linked 'theory' with medically oriented studies such as diagnosis. Theory and disease conditions were often compared and juxtaposed with basic nursing care, for example: 'When you first start all you do is basic nursing care, after that it is lost, all you do in other blocks is diseases; basic nursing care doesn't come back into it.'

There was also often an implied hierarchy in the terminology, 'just basic nursing care' compared with 'lumbar punctures and sterno-marrows as demonstrated and explained by doctors'. This is one of the many examples in the study of the dominance of the medical profession. The students appeared to be attracted by the lead taken by what Freidson (1970) has called the 'dominant profession' in health care. Knowledge which is linked with medicine is regarded as prestigious knowledge and therefore it is considered to be legitimate to draw upon it in order to bolster the status of nursing. Knowledge about 'just basic nursing' was not, it seems, regarded by the students in the same light. We shall return to the question of what might be considered to be legitimate and illegitimate knowledge upon which to base nursing status; the question will be discussed in relation to professionalism.

The data presented above provide examples of the mixed feelings of the students towards the role of 'theory' in nursing. One question which the data raises is: why have a large theoretical component in general nurse training? It seemed from the way in which the students used the word theory that it had a variety of meanings. Sometimes it meant the knowledge base upon which to found an activity, more commonly it was simply used to distinguish the parts of nursing which are taught in the college from those learnt on the wards. However, as we have already seen, theory was generally taken to mean medically oriented facts based on diseases and their signs and symptoms. There was an overall impression that the students saw nurse training in terms of a series of medically oriented lectures in the college, basic nursing picked up on the first wards, and some follow-up demonstrations of medical techniques, supplied presumably so that the student nurse becomes competent in assisting at these procedures. The professional dominance of medicine is reflected even in the nursing education programme.

Clearly, it is too simple an approach to reduce all nursing to a few categories which distinguish technical from basic care, with a view to specifying which of these tasks must be undertaken by trained, or at least learner nurses. The socio-psychological factors and the 'how is it carried out' aspects of nursing care are considered by many to be all-important. However, the fact remains that, according to the evidence of the students in this study, much of the nursing experience which they had was carried out in settings in which they could be seen to be interchangeable with the auxiliaries. Some of the students in the study discussed this interchangeability in terms of what it meant for professional nursing. One student said that nursing auxiliaries were doing more nursing work than they used to; 'they are coming into student territory – doing more and more things'. She gave as an example – auxiliaries taking patients' temperatures and pulses, and queried whether the auxiliary would note the quality as well as the rate of the pulse. 'We are taught to look for abnormalities and consequences, e.g. fibrillation – suppose that the charts were done by the auxiliary.'

Technical tasks are being sloughed off to the auxiliaries in much the same way that they were once passed from the doctor to the nurse. They have become low-prestige and routine tasks which nurses see fit to hand over to nursing auxiliaries, who are only trained in an *ad hoc* way to do whatever is required of them. As one student put it: 'given a good training by a ward sister they [auxiliaries] are good and valuable.' Hughes (1971:307) described how, in striving for professional status, nurses have tended to hand their work to 'aides and maids'. In this professionalizing effort, paradoxically, the nurses are taking over cast off medical work. This taking on and casting off should be undertaken with caution, as Johnson (1978) warns by quoting Augustus de Morgan (1872:377), who said: 'great fleas have little fleas upon their backs to bite 'em and little fleas have lesser fleas, and so ad infinitum.'

Why theory?

If one is going to argue that theory is an important part of nursing training and that it is important for patient care, a case has to be made for the utility of theory in terms of patient welfare, rather than in terms of successful professionalizing on the part of nurses. The question of interchangeability of students and auxiliary nurses could well damage the case for the former. In the case of the latter it could be suggested that the introduction of theory into what might otherwise be an essentially boring job serves to maintain the morale of the nurses and to attract intelligent people into the work.

First let us discuss the case for the utility of theory in nursing practice. If it is to be argued that all nurses need some training, currently a three-year programme, then there must be at least an economic, if not any other argument for maintaining this policy. If a cogent argument is to be put forward for training the current numbers of nurses, it must be the case that nursing care has to be carried out by trained personnel. Clearly, nursing care is not always undertaken by qualified staff; the majority of the nursing workforce comprises unqualified and untrained personnel, namely students and nursing auxiliaries. Nursing auxiliaries and learner nurses are at present working under supervision of a small number of trained staff. The whole system is dependent upon a constant stream of students presenting themselves for training each year. The process continues in this way because qualified staff are constantly leaving the workforce. The newly qualified staff nurses form a highly mobile population in that they move from post to post. There is also movement in and out of nursing, the most common reason being marriage and family. Employment of nurses has to be looked at, it must be remembered, in the wider context of the labour market and in the light of the changing role of women in society (Mercer 1979). Thus, the system continues to provide a large workforce of students and to lose a substantial number of trained staff, albeit temporarily.

What of the interchangeability of students and auxiliaries? One student described the operation of the student allocation policy on different wards. On the wards where there was a large student allocation, there were consequently few auxiliaries. Moreover, in such a situation the auxiliaries only help the nurses, 'they are really only nursing aides'. The students form a mobile workforce which can be shunted around the hospital as and when required. The auxiliaries can be seen as gap-fillers where there are not enough students allocated; a fact which exemplifies the interchangeability of students and auxiliaries. I put this type of argument to one student:

STUDENT: The NHS couldn't survive without auxiliaries, the publicity recently about not calling them nurses, etc. – I don't think it's justified. I learnt basic nursing care as an auxiliary [this student had spent several months as an auxiliary before starting training].

KM: You could argue that an auxiliary can do anything if shown.

STUDENT: They don't realize the implications, you should know why you do what you do, that's where the nurse comes into her own.

KM: Do you see that in practice or does she do no better than the auxiliary because when she gets into the ward she follows the routine instead of putting what she learnt into practice?

STUDENT: I think you can put it into practice, though you see a lot of bad practice in students and trained nurses [the implication being that there is not just bad practice from auxiliaries]. You see a lot of students who don't function well.

KM: If you put a set of students in to function routinely . . .

STUDENT: I actually find in some wards that the auxiliary will teach the basic nursing care. That's OK, with in-service training, they are taught more or less what we are taught in block. I don't know that it affects me that nurses are getting more responsibility but what would annoy me would be if I thought they were not doing it properly. I feel that auxiliaries are being given lists of their duties on more wards now because nurses feel that their territory is being encroached upon.

The above discussion is presented in order to demonstrate firstly, how the student nurse defended the auxiliaries' position, especially when I was seemingly attacking the auxiliary nurses' competence. It does seem, according to the students, that for the most part an auxiliary with limited, but focused training could undertake much of the routine basic care, under suitable supervision.

The arguments for a theoretically oriented nurse training seem to be aimed at the professionalization of nursing rather than the improvement of patient care. The questions of profession and professionalizing are addressed later. Mention is made here in order to establish a context for the worker/learner divide.

Student or worker?

The issue of how the students saw their role on the wards, that is in terms of being a learner or a worker, produced some interesting discussion, which relates, in part, to the whole question of profession. The main point is that if the student nurses can move from ward to ward in fairly rapid succession, find their way into an established routine and then proceed to care for patients in the manner prescribed by their seniors, with or without much more knowledge of the patient than the nursing auxiliaries have, can the end product of this training be a professional?

The distinction drawn from the data between student nurse as learner and as worker has some close connections with the differences between wards and the college of nursing. The learner–worker distinction has been singled out for separate attention because it does have some subtly different consequences. One student comment, which was very much to the point, sums the category up neatly thus: 'you just forget what you were taught in school and go ahead and work for the ward.' One student thought that even the qualified staff should do the 'basic tasks' because, 'that's nursing, at least what I see nursing as'. This led into a discussion of how she got along with the permanent staff:

STUDENT: SENs I get on really well with because they are in with the patients. Staff nurses I don't know, some of them I get on really well with but not on a working basis. They are giving you the orders, you run to them for help and that's it (. . .). When you first go on the ward they are really helpful, but if you don't progress as quickly as they think you should, they can turn round and be really nasty.

KM: Progress in what way?

STUDENT: Well, if you go on say your first ward and they think after, say three weeks, that you should know how to do things like bed bathing, observations and things like that, simple things, then if you are still incompetent in things like that then they can turn on you.

The student had been talking about the different ways of doing things on the different hospital wards. The emphasis seemed to be upon learning how the ward staff, or more properly, the ward sister liked things to be done. I raised the student/worker divide issue:

KM: (. . .) do you see yourself as a student who came here for an education, or do you see yourself as a worker?

STUDENT: A worker. You see, well both at the same time, but for instance, when you are in block, you definitely see yourself as a student and this is a good opportunity for you to learn; and when you are on the ward you are not only trying out what you have learnt, but you are taking in how that actually works, on a day-to-day basis. Also if you were just regarded as somebody there to learn, you picture a student nurse just standing there watching everything; whereas that obviously is no good, because you are part of the work team and especially in a medical ward you are there to pull your weight, just the same as the auxiliary or anybody, and if you don't they'll let you know about it. In that respect I think when you are on the wards sometimes you think, 'what is this, cheap labour, this is ridiculous', especially on some medical wards. On the other hand, there is no reason why you shouldn't be doing it. But you don't feel that you are being filled full of vitally important knowledge, the fact that you have been emptying bedpans for the last two hours and that Mrs X needs her bed changed again. It's both of them at the same time, but when you are on the ward you are a worker first but you are learning the work as you go along. It's hard to describe. I know what you mean (. . .). I don't see myself as being like a student, like a student at university, I see myself as being trained, but you are working as you are being trained, it's like an apprenticeship type thing. For that reason I think we are entitled to just as good a salary as anybody else that's pulling their weight and working hard.

This student's comments are quoted at length in order to illustrate the discussion of apprenticeship and nursing. The students' position is in some respects similar to that of an apprentice. One student actually differentiated between her status and that of a university, or 'real' student; and in doing so she employed the label apprentice. Yet the terms of the student nurse's apprenticeship are rather different from the traditional apprentice to craftsmen. The students move around frequently and can not be said to be apprenticed to 'masters', because of this mobility and because it seems that much of their time is spent working with auxiliaries. The medical students in the study by Becker *et al.* (1961:194) were seen to develop apprentice roles during their second year:

'The student does clinical rather than academic work. That is he gets his training primarily by working with patients rather than through lectures and laboratory work. . . . Though he remains in many senses a student he becomes much more of an apprentice, imitating full-fledged practitioners at their work and learning what he will need to know to become one of them by practising it under their supervision.'

The medical students were working with qualified doctors during this apprenticeship. In the case of student nurses, their 'craftsmen' should be the qualified staff with whom they work; yet, according to the students, they work much less frequently with trained staff than they do with other students and auxiliaries.

The quasi-apprenticeship nature of nurse training is shown in an interesting light when it is considered that much of the on-the-job learning happens between learners, senior 'apprentices' teaching junior 'apprentices' as it were. This teaching subculture is not altogether surprising when it is considered alongside the comments which the students made about their ability to function efficiently as workers. If the trained staff expect the students to pick up the 'job' in a short space of time and fill a vacant slot on the ward, whenever students need to know how to do something in order to function efficiently, they are more likely to seek help from a fellow apprentice than from a trained member of staff. This reliance on other students rather than on the qualified staff serves to point up the contradiction in the simple notion of a student apprenticeship.

Student nurses felt that the trained staff expected them to become efficient workers in quite a short space of time. This staff expectation can be seen as a consequence of the students being viewed as workers. It also demonstrates the kind of consequences of the worker/learner divide which go beyond the ward/college differences. This expectation is of interest on two counts. First, the student nurses are, by definition, learners and as such should not be expected to slip into full work roles immediately. Second, the very fact that the students move from ward to ward militates against their becoming efficient workers in a short space of time, because each time they achieve that state they are moved on.

The trained staff are the nurses on whom the students might model their behaviour. The students, however, complained that they did not often get a chance to work with qualified staff. Ward sisters sometimes spent their time in the office and so the students got few opportunities to see a ward sister working with patients. This was not always the case, one student said: 'you are very impressionable on your first ward, watch the sisters, these are the people you model yourself on.' Most of the students could remember one nurse, often a senior student, whose behaviour had impressed them. Another student said: 'In the first and second year you model yourself on others, if I was impressed by them, I acted like them – not so much now.' This same student said you could pick up a lot of different ways of doing things, and so she opted for the tutor's way. This presumably represented some constant force in the training.

One further aspect of the position in which student nurses find themselves has to do with the support which they receive during their training. Consider this student's comments:

KM: How do you get to know how you are getting on? Is there much feedback? I know you get an assessment on each ward, but on a day-to-day basis can you feel if you are any use to them?

STUDENT: You know yourself whether you have been in the way or are being helpful – the way they act towards you (. . .).

KM: Do you get any positive feedback if you are doing
           well, or is it just . . .
STUDENT: No, just if you are not doing well. Prefer a weekly
           assessment, not necessarily written but just to say 'you
           did well this week but do some work on your nursing
           care'. I think that a ward report is awful.
KM: It's a bit late anyway isn't it?
STUDENT: Yes, if they told you at the time you could change, it's
           just left and written in a report later.

Later, in a discussion of the differences between ward and college,
the same student went on to say that some of the things which are
acceptable on examination papers would be laughed at if mentioned on the ward. She did not think that this could be pointed out
to her tutor:

STUDENT: I don't like it, but that's the way they are [i.e. practical
           ward nursing and college teaching are different]. There
           is nothing you can do to change it unless you go to
           your tutor, knock on her door and have it out with her.
           I'm sure she'd be very chuffed [with sarcasm].
KM: [Pointed out that the worker/student divide was one of
           the analytic concepts which I was exploring at the
           moment.]
STUDENT: It is true, you don't like saying it to your tutors or they
           may say 'a trouble maker her you know'. They say
           'any problems you have, just come down'. Like my
           personal tutor, I couldn't tell him anything.
KM: Do you feel you get much support if, suppose you
           make a mistake (. . .) you said you get told off when
           things are wrong, and not told when they are well, do
           you feel that you are not really supported?
STUDENT: Well, if you do wrong, they let everybody know
           about it. Clinical teacher gets informed, get told to
           come up, they never come to see you. The nursing
           officer gets told and it gets written down in your thing
           [record].

The lack of support felt by the students was clearly associated with
their need for some feedback from the trained staff. One of the
strangest features of the apprenticeship was the reward system. A
student could often tell how she was progressing by the attitude of

the trained staff. 'If you are getting on OK the staff leave you alone, they don't really bother you.' This, according to one student, could sometimes be frightening, as she had more responsibility than she felt ready for; she also felt that this gave the trained staff an 'easy time'. It seemed that the reward for being a good apprentice, and appearing to be coping and 'getting on alright', was to be deprived of attention by the trained staff. Thus, the reward for good behaviour was no teaching. One student had difficulty in interpreting the reaction of the trained staff. When asked about feedback from the staff she said that she sensed her progress from what she was given to do. She saw it in terms of how far the trained staff trusted her, 'if left to myself they know I'll do it'. However, she did wonder if they were not 'just cutting corners and giving it to me because they can't be bothered to do it'. Her explanation, in the light of the fact that another student from her set never got the same amount of 'senior work' to do, was that 'I don't know if I get it because they don't like me, or because they trust me!' Such was the interpretation of the feedback received by this student.

Assessment and counselling

The students' need for feedback and some idea of how they are performing led to a consideration of the question of support for student nurses during training. The college of nursing has a system whereby each student has a personal tutor to whom they can go for help with academic or personal problems. It is interesting to note that there is no separation of the academic from the personal aspects of the tutor's role. A common practice in higher education is to have an academic tutor and a personal tutor, in some attempt to separate academic assessment of progress from personal affairs. Several students said that they would not go to their personal tutor if they had a problem. This was sometimes simply the result of personality differences. One student talked about the difficulties she had experienced in talking to patients about their diagnoses. She said that there could be no help from the college in these matters, it was much better and realistic if it came from the ward staff. I asked if the personal tutor could have been of any assistance, she said 'I don't think the tutor is much help, I wouldn't go to mine, tries too hard to be nice!' There was also a fairly general feeling among the students, typified in the above extract, that anything discussed with a personal tutor would be entered into the student's files and would work in some way against them.

The tutor's dual role of assessor and counsellor does not appear to be an acceptable, or credible, one from the students' perspective. The students were suspicious that counselling sessions might degenerate into assessment activities, resulting in negative information going into their files.

There were, however, very real problems facing the students and some coping mechanism is clearly needed. The following extracts illustrate their difficulties: 'I've become very cynical about life, more depressed than I used to be – now I've seen what can go wrong in life. . . . I think everyone is dying, everyone has got cancer, I have to go home to see friends, etc. who are not dying.' I asked her if she had any support over this in her training, for instance, did she feel that she was allowed to be upset. She said, 'No, just be a nurse and smile'. She did qualify this by saying that it depended upon who she was working with and how they reacted. Also, she found that talking to other students, both on the wards and in her own group, was of great help. Another student summed up the general need for support of students when she described her early days in nursing saying: 'The first couple of days especially, it's sheer hell – the last thing you can think of is how to reassure someone else, you want to be reassured yourself.'

The question of support for student nurses is raised again at various points in this analysis. In this context it seems that the support is being offered in a formal way by the college of nursing. Yet the students feel that support is needed on the wards. It therefore becomes a matter of chance and luck, depending upon who the student is working with, as to whether or not they get the desired help. The learner/worker divide is relevant here; on the wards student nurses are often regarded simply as workers and as such should be able to cope with their lot. The college of nursing sees the student as a learner and offers the personal tutor service accordingly. The students, balanced between these roles, often miss out on the support they need. Much of the problem, this analysis suggests, lies in the blurring of assessment and tutorial responsibilities both on the wards and in the college. The students felt unable to express any doubts or difficulties, for which they might reasonably expect advice and tutorial help, in case they simply got recorded and counted against them. This fear suggests that much more emphasis was laid, according to the students, upon assessment than on counselling and support.

Does the apprenticeship work?

In this chapter the dual status of student and worker has been examined. This divide is upheld structurally by the split which the students perceive between the college and the wards. The students were very ambivalent in their attitude towards this divide. There was a tendency to see both sides of the problem and in so doing they could neither reconcile the two nor come down in favour of one or the other. This is an important point, as it reflects the ambiguities which exist in nursing and which are clearly present in the students' nursing world. Perhaps the most striking revelation of the analysis is the notion that students and auxiliaries are interchangeable as part of the workforce.

The question of a need for theory in nursing in order to stimulate the student nurses in areas where the work is dull and repetitive is closely tied up with the idea of interchangeability of students and auxiliaries in the workforce. Braverman's notion of 'degraded work' is again pertinent. His argument, put briefly and it is hoped without doing it too much violence, states that as technology has advanced the labour processes have become at once sophisticated and tedious. Sophisticated because of the technology and detailed planning involved for one set of workers, and tedious because the work is broken down into small parts which require little or no skill to perform. 'Scientific managers' undertake the creative part of the process, whilst workers at the operational levels are left with the tedious aspects of the work. The literature reveals that the worker becomes alienated from the product of his labours and his work is as such deskilled and degraded.

The place of the craftsman in this process disappears. A comparison can be made to some degree with the situation in nursing. The 'scientific managers' are the trained staff, notably the ward sisters; the workers are all those who are not managers, namely the students and auxiliaries. The work is planned by the qualified staff and carried out by the unqualified. From this perspective the student nurse cannot be said to be an apprentice, she is not learning a skill from a recognized craftsman, rather she is working with a fragmented set of tasks which make up patient care. The price of the loss of craftsmen, conventional wisdom has it, is a lack of pride in the work and a lowering of standards. 'They [scientific managers] have not yet found a way to produce workers who are at one and the same time degraded in their place in the labour process, and also conscientious and proud of their work' (Braverman 1974:133).

Whilst this analogy should not be pushed too far as it serves merely to illustrate a tendency towards tedious, and other, work being carried out by untrained staff in nursing, it can be taken a little further. Drucker (1954:284) in a critique of 'scientific management' said: 'It does not follow that the industrial world should be divided into two classes of people; a few who decide what is to be done . . . and the many who do what and as they are being told.' Drucker went on to say that even the simplest of jobs should involve some planning. This, as Braverman points out, was not entirely a new idea, for Adam Smith once recommended 'education for the people in order to prevent their complete deterioration under the division of labour' (Braverman 1974:39).

The introduction of 'nursing care plans' and nursing according to the 'nursing process' (a problem-solving approach to nursing) could be seen as a means of introducing some decision making and planning element for the 'many' in nursing. Similarly the theory which goes into nurse training could be seen to serve the purpose put forward by Adam Smith. Indulgence in analogy can be taken so far as to miss the point of the argument. Clearly, it has to be remembered that nursing is a human service occupation and thus the forms of degradation, deskilling, and alienation, if indeed they occur, will not be so overt as their counterparts in industry. However, the general principle of enabling work to be done by the less skilled through the supervision of the qualified is one well recognized in achieving nursing work.

Braverman's discussion of the division of labour is set in the context of capitalist enterprise. The application of capitalist rationality was introduced into nursing by the Salmon Report of 1966 (DHSS 1966). Carpenter (1977) in a discussion of Salmon, describes the 'new managerialism and professionalism in nursing'. He says that Salmon 'explicitly called for a managerial structure based on the industrial model of professionalized management as under advanced monopoly capitalism'. This managerialism developed, in the main, at one level removed from direct patient care on the wards. Carpenter points out that in this formal structure, power, prestige, and remuneration are to be found to greater degrees the further away from patient contact one gets. Braverman's comment that only a small number of people require special knowledge (Braverman 1974:83) can be said to be true of nursing, if one looks at the ward sister, staff nurse, and auxiliary nucleus of permanent staff on each ward.

The students' complaint that they did not often get a chance to work with the trained staff is consistent with the deskilling argument, in so far as trained staff can be seen to be exonerated from simple forms of labour and hence it is left, by and large, to the student nurses. This is how nursing has been made to work. Throughout their training, nurses have been used to the notion of a nursing hierarchy on the ward. Those at the top are seen to be able to pick and choose what work they do, whilst those at the bottom must 'get the work done'. This system is perpetuated and justified by the fact that students pass up through the system to a position where they may, eventually, be more selective in the work they do. So it is not too surprising that student nurses are expected to come and go in the deskilled sector of the division of labour. Nor is it surprising, in the light of this analysis, that the students felt that they were evaluated according to their capacity to become efficient workers. Indeed, one might say that they saw themselves being evaluated as members of the workforce according to their competence as nursing auxiliaries.

4

NURSING IN THE DARK

The notion of 'nursing in the dark' emerged after a number of interviews during which students described their difficulties concerning what they could say to patients. The students complained that they were often left short of information, or, as some put it, 'in the dark', about patients' diagnoses. Moreover, the student nurses frequently did not know how much the patients themselves knew of their conditions; hence the idea of 'nursing in the dark' emerged. There is a wealth of nursing literature, particularly in the nursing press, which is devoted to communication with patients. Nurses are being exhorted to talk with patients, to explore their social circumstances, to nurse the whole patient, and so on. During these interviews it became apparent that there are very real barriers to this style of nursing inherent in the way nursing is organized on the wards.

There is room for a considerable amount of caution to be exercised in addressing the question of talking with patients. There is a tendency in popular writings on communication to take the view that a nurse is a nurse, even if she is a student nurse, and to expect a particular performance from 'the nurse' in terms of communication. At the very least it is probably worth saying that if students know how to avoid doing any untoward damage in their talk with patients they will have achieved a realistic goal. The students I spoke to made a very convincing case for treating the communication skill expectations that trained nurses have of students, and perhaps indeed of themselves, as far more problematic than it is currently the fashion to do.

One factor which appears to militate against student nurses talking freely with patients is the way in which information is handled by the senior staff on the wards. Also, as we have already seen, the expectations of the trained staff are such that the students felt that talking was not a legitimate activity, so long as there was physical work to be done.

There is a tendency for the ward report, which students receive at the start of a shift, to be brief and inadequate as a basis for their work. The following students' comments on this issue serve to illustrate the point:

STUDENT: You know sometimes, on some wards, you don't get a proper report about the patients and you don't feel safe sometimes – not because of your own knowledge but because you don't know what's going on in the ward. It's left to the senior nurses but the ones who have got to do the basic work, the student nurses, are not told properly; and you don't know what to say to patients when they ask things, just because you are not well enough informed about them. You've got to go and ask this and that one. And you know a patient turns round and says, 'I've got cancer' and you say 'have you?' or 'you haven't', you know, it's such that sometimes you don't even know. The ward that I'm in just now, you might not get a report for six or seven days.

In another interview a student said:

STUDENT: (. . .) the radiotherapy ward had sixty patients and I think seven doctors, you know, this sister couldn't be expected to come out onto the ward. She'd seven doctors rounds every morning or something, you know, what else could she do? But she was the type that hoarded the information and just let it leak out slowly to all of us. You know, it's very bad on a ward like that (. . .).

KM: How did you actually know what to do?

STUDENT: I had to keep rushing back and forward to senior members of staff – what should I do, what should I say, you know, patients lost a lot of faith.

KM: Did you have any sort of patient allocation, or 'those are your patients', 'you do those beds', anything like that?

STUDENT: Yes, she would likely say you work in that room and you'd have six patients and you'd honestly be going round thinking, I wonder what's wrong with this one. You know, cancer or what, and you maybe just had six patients but you knew very little about them, only what you could get out of the nursing care plan. And anyway, when you got a report on sixty patients it was, you know, Mrs so and so has such and such, sixty times; you know, I've lost what the first one had anyway.

KM: So did you feel that you nursed well on that ward?

STUDENT: Not really that well I don't suppose, I mean your nursing care was good from the point of pressure sores and that kind of thing, you know, but as far as knowledge of the patient and the patients' social circumstances you know, you know very little. You couldn't approach them even if you'd wanted to. It was just like going into cold water, you knew nothing. You know, you just started from scratch.

The above extracts point up not only the main feature, lack of information, but hint at the cause of this state of affairs. The senior nurses have the information yet do not pass it on to those who are in closest contact with the patients, namely the students. The students' lack of information leads, it seems, to further difficulties. When a student does not know all the facts of a patient's case, this, coupled with not knowing how much the patient knows, forces the student into an awkward position. She must cope with the situation by telling the patient something, whilst at the same time preserving her own position and saving face with the patients.

How much can the student say?

In short, the student suffers from at best, incomplete information and, at worst, absence of information. According to the students, this state of affairs is brought about largely by the way in which information is handled by the senior staff. The overriding impression was one of student nurses being left in the uncomfortable position of being front line workers with barely enough information to work on.

The students' accounts suggest that they believed that the trained staff were in possession of the information which they lacked. It is conceivable, however, that the trained staff were also 'in the dark' in some connections and were merely concealing this fact from the students by seemingly 'hoarding' the information. Alternatively the trained staff might be using uncertainty as a device for keeping students short of information. Davis (1960) used the term 'functional uncertainty' to describe how hospital staff can use real or pretended uncertainty in order to maintain control over the patients. Davis argues that doctors use this device when they are unclear about how they should proceed, yet do not wish to engender any lack of confidence on the part of the patient. Davis suggested that doctors used clinical 'functional uncertainty' in order to control their doctor–patient interactions. They declare their uncertainty of diagnosis whilst still conveying a competence which suggests that their patient management is reliable. The students that I interviewed could have been describing a version of this tactic which they had experienced at the hands of the trained staff on the hospital wards, 'functional uncertainty' this time being employed by the trained nursing staff as a means of retaining their power on the wards.

Aside from not knowing enough about the patient, the students often did not know what the patient had been told. Consequently, the students have to develop strategies for coping with this information gap, strategies which often involve evasion and a guarded approach to nursing. The following extracts illustrate the students' position:

STUDENT: (. . .) you have to play ignorant, you know, you say 'I'll get someone to speak to you about it', which is really bad because they may have plucked up a lot of courage to tell you. You have to have a staff nurse or a sister come and speak to them about it, you know, it would be good if they had better communication between some senior members of staff, you know, they seem to hoard all the information and nobody gets to know it.

KM: Because even if you have to say 'I'll get sister', you could at least appear as if you knew the situation instead of wondering 'what is she going to ask me next?' Does it alter your behaviour towards the patients at all, when you are not sure what they know about their condition or what you can say to them?

STUDENT: Yes, like on the radiotherapy ward, it's who knows what, they are always anxious to know what it does

(. . .). The few times they have asked me you can always sort of palm it off, 'I'm not very sure', or 'I can ask sister'. It's amazing the people who don't realize that radiotherapy is a treatment for cancer you know.

Another student said:

STUDENT: (. . .) there could always be more communication but on the other hand, there are so many reasons why there can't be. I hate to go on about short staffing but sometimes, the time when the patient is actually really needing someone to go and talk to him just happens to be the time when no one has got the time, and later on when somebody has got the time they are not ready to talk about it (. . .).

KM: Have you found that you have been kept in the picture sufficiently with what's going on to be able to tell the patients what they want to know (. . .)? It has been suggested at some of the earlier interviews that junior nurses have been the ones that have been closest to the patients and the patients will tend to ask them. But often they haven't been told, say, whether a patient knows his diagnosis or whether he has talked to anybody about it. How have you found this?

STUDENT: Well I don't think there is enough, I don't know if *any* of the students get to know any more, I don't think it's just junior nurses, I think it is probably the other students as well. But on the other hand there are some things that they will tell the more senior students but they just sort of brush it off as if to say 'oh you don't need to know about that', with a non-stripe. As you say, it is true that people do ask you more, the junior nurses get asked.

KM: And how do you find that to handle?

STUDENT: You do feel ignorant, you do feel that you don't really know enough about this person to really judge it for yourself what you should say.

KM: Which seems to be what people are saying, you are short of information anyway, just simple things, that the doctor might have said to the patient and you just don't know whether he has or not.

STUDENT: That's right.[1] One patient asked me if he was dying. I
said 'Oh, don't be silly, you're doing fine' or something like that. Whereas I had a pretty good idea that
he wasn't going to live, I was not absolutely positive
and also I wasn't sure whether anybody had spoken to
him or anybody had spoken to his relatives, whether
anybody had actually said anything concrete or not.
Although I think most people would not actually
reassure and say 'you are doing fine', not say 'you
definitely will live' but 'you are doing fine' or
something like that as an easy way out because you
don't want to take the responsibility on yourself for
saying, 'you are going to die tomorrow', 'or 'you are
not going to live'.

KM: Especially when you haven't been told anything.

STUDENT: Especially when you haven't been told anything, you
don't know where you are. I think that is very
important, again I don't think that is just the junior
nurses, I think maybe the sister knows maybe the
doctor won't have told anybody, you just don't know
where you are; or they maybe have spoken to the
relatives and told them that they are going to die but
have not told the patient, so the patient isn't supposed
to know that the relatives know but you don't know
who knows. So what if the relatives come up to you
and say 'how long do you think he has got?' and you
say, 'oh, he is doing fine' but the doctor has told them
that he is dying (. . .). I think we have to be a team
anyway, between medical and nurses and I think if you
have come to a conclusion about something everybody should be put in the picture and then also told
what is to be done about it, the doctor decides that the
patient isn't to be told, then OK fair enough, that is up
to him to decide because it is his responsibility, but lets
all of us know what is going on (. . .). So you are not
only put in embarrassing situations but you might
make a mistake.

---

[1] Note that I had asked for a simple example of information lack.

The first student said that she would 'play ignorant' in order to avoid having to answer a patient's question which she was ill-equipped to answer. She felt that, if the senior staff were to keep the juniors more informed and not 'hoard' the information, life might be easier for the student nurses. The second student, quoted above, highlighted the general aura of uncertainty which surrounds the question of talking to patients. The problems which the student nurses face are quite acute, as they constantly encounter patients who may or may not know their diagnoses. Questioning of the students by these patients can be difficult because sometimes the student has no way of knowing whether the patient simply wants to discuss what he already knows or if he is seeking information about his diagnosis. It is interesting to note that whilst the students gave the impression that lack of information caused, in the main, small, irritating, day-to-day problems, when they gave an example it was invariably a dramatic one of diagnosis disclosure. It might be argued that this kind of 'dramatic' event occurs much more frequently in the students' imagination and anticipation of problems, rather than in their actual experiences. The stress which comes from 'nursing in the dark' is much more likely to stem from the ever present threat of a patient saying 'am I going to die?' rather than from the student actually experiencing such a question. I gained the impression that the 'does he know?' encounters which the students recalled were very much part of their student 'story-swapping' practice. It is probable, therefore, that a kind of folklore grows which keeps alive the dramatic side of nurse–patient encounters, yet which bears little resemblance to their daily ward work.

The student nurses' position in the hospital hierarchy has important implications for the ways in which they can handle the situation in which they are placed. Students are junior, unqualified, members of the workforce and as such invariably have to follow specific orders or the general policy of the ward. The students often expressed their own personal views on whether patients should be told the truth. They did, on the whole, though, recognize that there had to be an 'official line' to follow; the formulation of this line was generally considered to be the responsibility of the medical staff.

The student quoted above made it quite clear that she was willing to follow the 'official line' but had difficulty in determining what it was because information was hoarded by senior staff. The following extract puts the other side of the coin, although this student concedes that an 'official line' is necessary.

STUDENT: (. . .) Most of the patients in my ward have got multiple sclerosis and things like that. There should be a policy where you know where you stand with these people; you can't possibly support them if they know they've got something nasty and they are just waiting for you to tell them they've got something nasty, exactly what it is. It's really weird, they ask you these questions, you've got to be so much on your guard in case you say something.

KM: (. . .) This is something which has been brought up, until now, by more junior students – about them being really on the spot because they are always doing the basic care and the patients will say to them 'what about this?' and they never know whether they are being played off against somebody else, whether they [the patients] really don't know or whether they don't want to hear. And quite often the student doesn't know what to say anyway, because she doesn't know (. . .).

STUDENT: Well, I've got to the stage where I know if I'm played off against somebody else, usually, unless it's my first day on a ward. Just the way the patients phrase things and that, and usually you just try to be truthful. I'm totally against people sort of adopting this sort of optimistic kind of thing, it's so characteristic of a lot of nurses, you know. 'You're going to be alright', or 'that wound looks lovely' when the thing looks absolutely revolting, really. I think that's terrible. Any patient with half an IQ will see through that. It is possible I think to sort of strike a happy medium with a patient and just listen to him saying very little. You know, they say something like 'I think I might have got cancer' you just say 'oh, yes there is always this possibility but you must wait for the results of your tests'. Whereas they [the nurses she referred to] say 'oh, no, no, you can't have cancer' – that's ridiculous because the patient is bound to feel they are thinking they have got it until they are proved wrong.

This student believed that patients should be given the facts. However, the policy of the consultant was not always to tell the patient and so she felt that she had to follow the official line. This was possible so long as the policy was clear, although, in general, she said that when possible she tried to be truthful. She felt that it was possible to adopt a 'happy medium' approach and usually just listened and said very little. In contrast though, another student said that she had difficulty in handling situations where she was not allowed to tell a patient about his condition when he asked. She thought that if a patient asked a nurse about his condition, and the nurse knew the diagnosis, she should be able to say something. This rather spirited approach to disclosure was not common among the students. On the whole, they were content to follow the policy of the consultant in charge of the case so that the patient got a story which was, at least, consistent if not accurate.

The following student's comments exemplify this. In discussing talking with patients the question of who should give information arose:

KM: (. . .) Would you say that it is part of the nurse's role, rather than the doctor's side of things?

STUDENT: No, I would say it was the doctor's side. Because if a patient is going to be told something it's better coming from a doctor or a surgeon rather than a nurse, unless the nurse has been specifically told to tell the patient. It sounds better coming from a doctor than it would do a nurse.

This latter approach points up the implication which the issue has for nursing's claim to 'profession'; we will return to this. Meanwhile, it is interesting to note the students' acceptance of a subordinate position for nursing in relation to medicine in the area of communication. This subordination is only one example, among many, of the prevailing medical dominance which makes nursing's claim to professional status problematic.

Evasion

Even when the students accepted and followed an 'official line' they experienced difficulties in doing so. The students complained that they had to be evasive with patients and, on occasions, to use their expression, to 'fob them off'. The student cited below had some difficulty in describing how she decided what to say to patients and eventually conceded that patients were often 'fobbed off'.

KM: Do you think it helps when you know a bit more about the patient? You often hear younger nurses are frightened that a patient will ask them something that they have not got the answer to (. . .).

STUDENT: Basically, if a patient asks you something you just, I don't know, I never really think about that. Most people say that they don't know, on the whole, so you ask somebody else and they go, or you say I'll get so and so to speak to you – if you don't know anything. I think basically it's still the same now [i.e. she is a more senior student] you maybe tell the patient what you think they should know. It depends upon what they know already, it depends on what they have, what's wrong with them, how much you tell them, and how much you fob them. It's true you fob people quite a lot in nursing. (. . .) It is difficult (. . .) when you know more than they know. It's difficult to cope with.

KM: Yes, especially if you do not know how much they know.

STUDENT: And you think they must know something, or more than I think they know. And actually, they are testing you, fishing for extra bits of information. It is difficult to know really unless you have been told directly how much they know, you tend to fob them then until you know exactly what they know.

KM: And how do you feel when you are doing the fobbing?

STUDENT: Terrible sometimes, but you are told it is not your decision as to how much your patient knows in the situation so you fob them off. But you don't like it because you look at the patient and you think, you are a human being and you are entitled to know because it is your life.

The discussion then moved towards how the information giving could be handled on the wards. More specifically, how updating of information should be carried out.

STUDENT: I think the staff should be told at the report, at lunch time – tell you then. I think basically the whole staff should know.

KM: Then everybody has the same.

STUDENT: The same grounding to know how to fob the patient
             off or how to deal with them if they ask you.

KM: I was just wondering, you said you felt awful to keep
             fobbing them off. Do you think that if it was more
             organized, in that you knew everybody was doing it,
             that it was the thing to do, would you feel any better
             about it?

STUDENT: Probably, that you were not the only one that was
             totally fobbing them off; I mean, you knew that they
             were going to have the same story.

KM: Whilst you were fobbing them off was there, possibly,
             the worry at the back of your mind that you were
             doing something different anyway?

STUDENT: That somebody is going to come along and tell them
             something else? Probably, I think so, but you see, I
             think you would be a lot better if you knew everybody
             was doing the same. Then it would just seem like a wee
             white lie, but you're really fobbing them off.

It appears that the students were forced to be evasive with the
patients for three main reasons. Firstly, because they often lacked
the necessary information; secondly, they did not know how
much the patient knew of his condition; and thirdly, because they
had been instructed not to tell the patients anything. Clearly, the
third situation is the least problematic of the three. If a consultant
does not wish a patient to be told the diagnosis, then the nursing
staff are not in a position to ignore this decision. The question of
lack of information is rather more complex. Whether the student is
not in possession of the relevant facts, or does not know how much
information the patient has, is a matter of practical as well as
analytic interest. The student has the problem of handling the
situation in either case, though the tactics used and the difficulties
encountered will differ.

The students expressed a fear of telling a patient something
which he did not already know. The general confusion about who
knew what made this a real problem. The students, especially
junior ones, found themselves working closely with patients about
whom they sometimes knew very little and still less about the
patient's own insight into his condition. If a patient asked a
question about his diagnosis, the students were not always in a

position to know whether he was 'fishing' for further information, which the medical staff had seen fit to deny him or whether he was simply trying to discuss his condition.

This question of 'who knows what' has been described by Glaser and Strauss (1965) in terms of 'awareness contexts'. They developed the notion of awareness contexts in their study of the events and activities which surround dying patients, their relatives, and the hospital staff. For instance, when the staff and the relatives know that a patient is dying, yet the patient does not know, Glaser and Strauss describe the situation as one of 'closed awareness'. They describe three other types of awareness contexts: 'open awareness', when the patient and relatives know that he is dying, 'mutual pretence' and 'suspicion awareness' are the terms used to describe situations when both parties know the situation, but pretend not to, and where one party knows the situation and the other only suspects. The notion of 'awareness contexts' is applicable to the present study in the interpretation of the students' description of information handling. The students were essentially describing what Glaser and Strauss would call a 'closed awareness context', where the patients did not know the facts. The students often shared this context in their dealings with the trained staff, that is to say the trained staff were aware and the students were not. Indeed, the students felt that in some cases the patients knew more than they did and were simply looking for additional information or confirmation of what they already knew. 'Suspicion awareness' might describe such situations.

It is not the intention here to fit my findings into the categories drawn up by Glaser and Strauss, rather to use their work to highlight the uncertainty which surrounds the whole business of student nurses talking with patients. The uncertainty both of their own knowledge and that of the patient seemed to be the crux of the problem facing the students. The lack of information of which the students complained was not always crucial life and death information. If students are not kept up to date about what a patient knows and does not know about his condition it can make nursing and talking with him a delicate business. Because of the prevailing awareness context a student's construction of a conversation might be very different from the patients. The student quoted above talked about patients 'testing' you and fishing for extra bits of information. The answers which she gives a patient are thus dictated by her perception of this request for information. Just as the patient has little control over the nurse's interpretation of his remarks, so the nurse has little control over the patient's interpretation of hers. It might be that the student nurses create an impression of conspiracy for the patient when the facts of the matter are that they, quite simply, don't have the answer. Patients may read ominous meanings between the innocent lines of a student's evasive reply to a question. Where there is uncertainty and a lack of facts the chances of misunderstandings occurring are likely to increase. Thus, it could be argued that the uncertainty involved in 'nursing in the dark' caused more of the problems for student nurses than did the actual lack of information.

Uncertainty

It is interesting to note here that, whilst uncertainty is seen to complicate the student nurse's life, it has been shown to be of positive use to doctors in their dealings with cancer patients. McIntosh (1977) found that doctors used uncertainty as a means of limiting the degree of disclosure to patients. Davis (1960), as we have seen, uses the notion of 'functional uncertainty' to describe how doctors declare their lack of certainty, thus enabling the medical profession to manage and limit its interaction with patients. McIntosh suggested that uncertainty was used in a subtle way in his study, so that it was alluded to rather than openly professed. McIntosh (1977:67) describes how doctors used euphemistic terminology such as 'nasty cells' and 'activity' which does not, in itself, imply uncertainty.

'The use of this sort of terminology also solved a potential dilemma for the doctor: namely how could he use a pretence of uncertainty to restrict information while at the same time conveying to the patient that he knew what he was doing? The method adopted was, as we have seen, to use terms which, while implying uncertainty in sufficient degree to allay patients' fears, also avoided a more explicit profession of it. The doctors could not openly profess to be uncertain about the diagnosis, after having completed their investigations, without the risk of losing the patient's confidence in their ability to treat them. But, the use of terms like "suspicious cells" displayed appropriate combination of uncertainty and confidence in what they were doing to convince the patient that, whilst they might not be certain of the precise nature of their condition, they were sufficiently conversant with it to be able to treat it effectively.'

This extract underscores the subordinate position of nursing *vis-à-vis* the medical profession when it comes to communicating with patients. The doctor is able to use information and the lack of certainty in its presentation as a means of control of and power over patients. He is able to function in a comfortable fashion because he is in control of the 'line' that the patient is given. Furthermore, he spends far less time with the patients, and probably exercises a greater degree of control over any interaction with patients than can the student nurse. On the other hand, such 'uncertainty' leaves the patient full of questions which he is very likely to ask the nurse – often the student nurse. In the wake of such a complicated and subtle communication pattern of the medical staff, the student nurse is left with both the patient's received uncertainty from the doctor and her own uncertainty which stems from a lack of information about what has gone before.

McIntosh (1977:71–7) suggests that the nurses were 'in a position, had they wished, to bring the doctors' efforts at communication management to nought'. In contrast to the students' accounts in this present study, McIntosh found that the nurses were 'kept well informed about the patients' diagnosis and treatment'; they were thus potential sources of the information which the patients desired. He does, however, state that: 'Junior nurses had much less experience of what the medical staff told patients, primarily because they often lacked the opportunity to acquire it.' The nurses, McIntosh found, gave the same reasons as the medical staff for not telling patients, namely, 'they believed that patients did not want to know'. This statement might, however, beg the question, from where do the nurses take their lead in arriving at this opinion? McIntosh suggests that the nurses 'feared that distressed and agitated patients would make life more difficult for them'. It might also be further evidence of the dominant position of the medical profession.

The students clearly did not like having to be evasive in their dealings with the patients. The students' position is at once eased and compounded by the fact that they have no control over it. If they are told 'not to tell' then they must not; if they are not given information, their position is such that it is difficult to obtain. Yet they are placed in a position of having to do something when the patient asks his question. The fact that the students' position is not one which they adopt voluntarily does not make the evasion and the 'fobbing off' any easier to come to terms with.

One student, who admitted to answering questions in as vague a way as possible, seemed to take refuge in the fact that she had no choice about being evasive with the patients. Her description of answering patients' questions was unique among the students interviewed. It is cited here in order to throw the main argument of this chapter into relief. The majority of the students expressed concern about the restrictions placed on their talking with patients. This student had a rather different attitude:

KM: How do you feel about the nurse's role in giving information, how have you found it?

STUDENT: Well, at the moment I try to be as vague as possible and pass it on to the sister (. . .). I try to be as vague as possible you know, put it down in as broad terms as possible. Well, if they have an obstruction, well they want to know what an obstruction is, you just tell them it's something that's clogging their insides up. And if they ask what is it – what is clogging my insides up – just say – could be anything from constipation – millions of things can clog you up. And I have found in my experience so far that that more or less satisfies them, knowing that you can't boil it down to one particular thing or if there are still tests being run on them – just say 'I don't know, we haven't got the results of the tests'. Then tell ward sister or whoever is in charge at that time – that they have been asking – and what I have said so that they are in the picture in case somebody else gets asked and that it slips out. You know – it keeps you in the clear because as sure as fate they're bound to come up and say who else has been asked. It keeps you in the clear but at the moment I try to be as vague as possible and pass it on to the ward sister.

This student, apart from seeming to be content with evasion and vague explanations, made a practice of telling the ward sister what she had said in order to 'keep in the clear'. This style of handling the patient's question, whilst not typical, did seem to offer a solution to the problem of truthful communication. Indeed, viewed in this way the problem did not exist.

Not all students were prepared to be evasive. There was, even so, a reluctance to admit to complete ignorance when a patient asked a question.

STUDENT: If I don't know then I'll tell them I don't know the answer and I'll find out for them rather than fob them off with something.

KM: And have you always been like that, when you were a junior and you really didn't know, or probably knew a lot less about things and it happened to you more often?

STUDENT: I think then rather than just say you didn't know directly, say you weren't very sure.

KM: I've often wondered if there is something in nurses that they are always supposed to do everything, the public see them as, well, I don't know what they see them as, but they can cope with any situation and you are rather taught a little bit that way, I just wonder how, when a patient asks something, is it easy for a nurse to say 'I don't know'.

STUDENT: No, because, well it depends on what they ask you, but they tend to look at you as if you are stupid if you don't know the answer. I think it is better to say 'I'm not really very sure', than spin a yarn of what you think it might be, then find out.

Another student:

KM: Do you find that you have to kind of hedge your bets sometimes if you don't know what the medical staff have told them?

STUDENT: Mm, you have got to kind of, you . . .

KM: How do you deal with that?

STUDENT: You go round about it in a very non-commital way. I think you just try and make your patient feel that you have answered the question, you know, saying that you will check and try and get the doctor to speak to them as well. Tell them something that's going on, if you can (. . .) you feel pretty useless if you really don't know. Once or twice I've had to say 'I'm sorry, I just

> really don't know what's going on but I'll find out for
> you'. You feel that you are lacking.

It appears from the above extracts that, alongside the strategies for
coping with nursing on the basis of scanty information, the
students had to find ways of 'face saving' when they were in
awkward situations. Student nurses seem to find difficulty in
admitting when they do not know something. The ideal image of
a nurse, who can cope, knows all the answers, and is always
efficient, is, in some way, seen as a grail to strive for.

Clearly, if students are often deprived of the necessary information required to function in the front line, and, furthermore, do
not like to admit when they do not know, there are times when
student nurses find the work very stressful. Student nurses are
exposed to the worst side of life at quite a young age, and have to
cope the best way they can. As it has been argued, the students felt
that there was a move away from the patients as they become more
senior. This leaves the junior students, to a greater extent, in the
front line. These students are least well equipped to cope, by virtue
of being short of confidence and experience, less knowledgeable
than their seniors and, for the most part, the youngest nurses on the
ward. Also, the junior students do not have the status, nor the
permanence, which would help them to function in this front line
position. Without trying to explain their position in too deterministic a way, it does seem that, because a student is seen to be a
junior, and one who is just passing through the ward, she cannot
hope to carry off her duties in the same style that a senior student or
staff nurse might. Nevertheless, patients do commonly turn to the
junior nurses because they are the members of the nursing staff that
the patients encounter most frequently.

The following extract seeks to illustrate some of the points of the
above discussion.

KM: How do you find talking with patients, do you find it
           easy?
STUDENT: At first I found it very difficult, but I think that was
           because I was very shy and hadn't had much ex-
           perience so obviously as I've got more into nursing and
           I've become more confident, more able to talk freely,
           also as I've become more senior, it gives you a feeling
           of confidence when you are talking to them (. . .) felt

very junior and very inferior, which I don't feel so much now. I feel more on an equal basis, with anybody.

KM: How do you feel about information-giving?

STUDENT: That's quite important especially nowadays. I was quite surprised at how much patients knew about their condition (. . .). Patients do ask you a lot and they do ask you awkward questions.

KM: How do you find that, do you always know what the medical staff told patients or are . . .

STUDENT: You are sometimes left in the lurch (. . .).

KM: How do you deal with it if you are in the lurch, as you say, because you never know?

STUDENT: I'd refer it to somebody senior to myself [laughs].

KM: Which is presumably no bad thing, because you could be in a position where a patient is asking you to say something that he hasn't yet been told, whose responsibility is that (. . .)?

STUDENT: I would never tell a patient something that I didn't think that the doctor hadn't already told him. I would refer it to someone more senior, e.g. charge nurse, because it is the medical staff's responsibility and if they pass it over to the nursing staff then it's the nurse in charge of the ward's responsibility. Because right now I don't feel that I'm capable of telling somebody that they have cancer or that a relative has passed on. I don't know how I'm going to take to that because I almost got left with it once and it is very frightening because I wouldn't have known what to say.

KM: (. . .) in a few months time when you are a staff nurse and you do get landed with this (. . .)

STUDENT: I don't know how I'm going to react, I suppose I'll jump that bridge when I come to it.

This student felt subordinated as a junior nurse. As a second year student now she cannot envisage telling any patient that he has, say, cancer. When asked how she felt that she would cope when she became a staff nurse and had to do these things, she said that she 'would jump that bridge when I come to it'. This, rather flippant, answer is nearer to the truth than many might care to admit. The question of anticipatory socialization, or how students can adapt to and learn the staff nurse role before actually occupying it, is discussed elsewhere but comments such as the one above serve to emphasize the point that this type of socialization is not prevalent in nursing.

Establishing a 'professional' relationship

How, then, does the junior nurse learn to handle her role? This chapter has been concerned with the students' description of talking with patients. We must now examine how qualified staff acquire their various skills, particularly those for establishing a 'professional' relationship with the patient. A number of the students said that they watched senior staff at work and copied their approaches to the patients. This was not always considered to be enough, as evidenced by the student quoted below.

STUDENT: I don't think we get enough in our training, enough sort of formal education on how to speak to folk. We get psychology lectures but nothing really on how to just sit down and speak to somebody. The other day I was put in a situation when a patient was dying and nobody expected her to die, sort of thing. As soon as she did, and at the time there were six of her relations round the bed when she sort of took her last breath, and they all broke down, and everything. . . . And I sort of suddenly realized I was in that situation and I thought 'oh heck – what do I do now?' I ushered them off and made them a cup of tea and asked if there was anything I could do – and . . . Even if you did have formal education in how to speak to folk, I don't think you can until you have come up against it.

This example is rather 'dramatic', yet it serves to illustrate the position in which the students find themselves. She made the point that little formal instruction is given which might help the students in these situations, but went on to say that in any case she doubted the utility of such instruction. It seemed that, whilst the students would like some guidance and reassurance as to the efficacy of their actions, they are mostly resigned to the 'baptism by fire' which they experience. The student still has the problem of a lack of qualified nurse status when she is being asked to carry out work which, it could be argued, is more properly the concern of the trained staff. The data allow no more than a few discursive remarks. I suggested to the student quoted below that the students were in a difficult position when it came to establishing a 'professional' relationship with patients. They are seen by the patients as students and, as such, might not be viewed in the same light as, say, the sister or staff nurse might be. This led on to a discussion of how the relationship is founded.

STUDENT: (. . .) you have to show that you are a friend to them, that you are willing to be a friend first and that they can rely on you to help them, to show that you are interested in them as people.

KM: How do you find that, it was interesting that you used the word friend. Is there any difference between that and the professional image of the nurse? I'm interested in just how you go about making a relationship with people.

STUDENT: Well of course you still have to have a professional attitude but, on the other hand, I don't think anybody wants to be seen as a starchy person, they want to see that you are human but that you are capable of doing certain things in a professional manner. That they can depend on you to give them the right help that they need but without being a complete alien special kind of person, that you can't communicate with.

KM: So, would you say a friendly professional?

STUDENT: Yes.

KM: I wondered too a little bit about how you manage to develop that as a junior nurse. How do you go about it because you are at a bit of a disadvantage if the patient is going to think 'she has only just started'.

STUDENT: Well, I think it is also an advantage in a way. I think that it is easier for the junior to show that you're accessible as a person because the patients are not really expecting you to do anything terribly technical or anything right from the first word. Also you are nervous too and you want to make friends, you know, have a friendly basis with people, you don't want to be scowling and hiding and thinking everyone is thinking you are a fool for not knowing something. I find it quite easy to talk to people anyway and I'm usually quite cheery on a ward. I think if they see you singing or something like that, smiling or joking they think 'oh what a nice friendly type of girl' and that brings down the doubts that you might have that you might be a sadist or something (. . .). I think it is just your general attitude on the ward and your way of speaking to the other nurses as well and also how they treat you – I think gives them an idea of what type of person you are (. . .).

'Professional' was the word used by the students in order to describe the nature of the relationship with the patients which they felt was appropriate. There seemed to be two main opinions expressed by the students in relation to the ease with which students could establish a relationship with the patient. One argument is that the student can only try out her qualified nurse role, and its appropriate behaviour, when she is a qualified nurse. The other maintains that the junior student is closer to the patient and can, therefore, develop a friendly relationship with patients, who, in turn, will not expect too much of her, precisely because of her junior position. A further complication exists for the student who wishes to copy the behaviour of senior staff. This lies in the fact that role-modelling has its limitations in so far as when a ward sister or staff nurse speaks to a patient or answers his questions, she does so from a particular status position which the patient recognizes. The patient sees this as the sister's province. To make a crude analogy just as he might expect his bedpan from the junior student, so he expects his information from the qualified staff. In some ways, therefore, it matters less how the information is passed, than by whom it is passed. This fact makes it difficult for students to learn these skills as they can only really get it right when they have the necessary accompanying status.

The students, on the whole, expressed a willingness to talk with patients. Indeed, in some cases, they were almost over eager to discuss delicate issues with patients. There seems to be a tension between the students' belief that a patient has a right to know and their lack of ability to talk openly with patients. This tension is resolved by the students' accepting that the doctor has responsibility for determining what his patient should know. Also, in practice, the students were often either kept 'in the dark' or told 'not to tell'; in this way their desire to give the patients the truth was curbed if not resolved.

'Nursing in the dark' raises important issues concerning how far the student nurses should be treated as members of the ward staff. It seems that they are expected to function as full members of the workforce yet they do not have either the experience or the responsibility to go with it. Students are in a permanent dilemma as front line workers. They are taught in college that to talk with patients is an important part of care; yet on the ward this is made difficult, if not impossible, because of the way in which the information is handled by the senior staff. This state of affairs is, by and large, overlooked in the growing literature on nurse–patient communication: an examination of the context in which communication takes place would make a useful addition to that literature.

5

JUST PASSING THROUGH

So far we have examined different aspects of the students' experiences of becoming nurses. This chapter looks at the notion of transience, as it is one of the main features of the student's life. The students are constantly on the move from ward to ward as they gain the requisite number of hours' experience in different areas of nursing practice. 'Just passing through' was an expression used by one of the students during the interviews, and it adequately sums up the nature of the student experience. From the start of training most of the encounters which the student has are circumscribed by place and time and are, invariably, short-lived. The placements in various hospital wards and departments, spells of experience in hospitals, other than the main training hospital, and periods of time in the community are all arranged around blocks of weeks spent in the college of nursing. This fragmentation of the three years means, in effect, that the students I interviewed moved on average every eight or ten weeks.

The notion of transience first came to my attention in the consideration of the data concerned with the students' adjustment to the different expectations of the ward sisters. In the course of the interviews, the students made few specific references to the fact that they moved from place to place, possibly because they took this aspect of their life for granted. Nevertheless, there were many indirect references to this ephemeral facet of student life.

Broadly, it can be said that the transient nature of the students' encounters leads to several consequences for the students themselves, the permanent staff and, necessarily, the social organization of nursing on the wards. I shall argue that the students utilize transience in order to 'get through' their training. It allows them to escape long term responsibility for their actions because they form a moving population of workers, with some claim to student status. The following extract touches upon many issues and in so doing provides an overview of the problems of transiency. This student wanted to move on to another hospital in order to see different ways of nursing.

STUDENT: I'm [X] Hospital-orientated and to me there is no other 'right' way of doing a bed bath, or right way of doing this; and I'd like to see other ways.

KM: Do you find that there are routines that are hospital-wide, does it feel like a hospital or a collection of wards?

STUDENT: Well, like certain procedures you have a procedure manual and every ward does it exactly the same way.

KM: What kind of things differ from ward to ward?

STUDENT: Bed bathing obviously differs.

KM: What, when you do it, or how?

STUDENT: When and how you do it. Talking to your patients differs in different wards (. . .) the sister sets her guidelines, it's her ward, her domain, and you do not interfere.

KM: Do you feel as a moving student population through the wards? Do you feel an outsider?

STUDENT: You do feel an outsider, my staff [i.e. the staff on her present ward] makes you feel like that.

KM: What about working with auxiliaries, are they nearer to you or staff?

STUDENT: They are nearer to senior staff, because they are there all the time (. . .). Auxiliary nurses should be changed from ward to ward, if they get into a (. . .) niche with the sister on the ward. If you take a dislike to an auxiliary or they take a dislike to you they can make your life misery because they take back to the senior staff – they come back to you (. . .). I would move them around if I had my own way. I think sisters should move, I wouldn't allow them to get into their own sort of rut. I think if you moved a surgical sister to a medical department, she wouldn't have a clue, and that is wrong because you are obviously getting out of contact with one aspect of nursing and just sort of staying in your own wee cupboard.

KM: Do you not think that it is a bit inevitable?

STUDENT: I don't see why it can't be changed. I don't see why they can't be rotated on a two-yearly basis or something. Giving them long enough to get into a ward, to put in her ideas, her way of thinking and then changing her. Also it would work in a profitable way for students (. . .).

The student quoted above appeared to have accepted the transient nature of her work. Indeed, she implied that transiency was conducive to good nursing practice and advocated that it should be extended to all nursing staff, in particular to ward sisters and auxiliaries. This is not an uncommon practice. It is, for example, a part of military life.

'Getting on' and 'getting through'

There are two other main points to be drawn from the extract. First, the nature of the relationship established between the student and permanent staff on the ward seemed to be an important factor in determining whether a student enjoyed her period of time on any particular ward. Second, the students were aware of having to 'fit in' with the 'ways of the ward'. Most of the students described this need to adapt their behaviour, as they moved from one ward to the next, to meet the expectations of the sister and the permanent ward staff. The following extract illustrates the point.

KM: How do you find that you get on with the trained staff, as a student moving around every ten weeks (. . .)?

STUDENT: As a new student on the ward you get really depressed because, I think, even before you begin to think about the patients and how you are going to treat the patients you begin to think – 'just as long as I settle into the ward, get on with the staff'. That's the most important thing. You become very two-faced you know, really, you're doing some things and doing other things just to get on with the staff; and once you've been accepted by them, then you begin to think more about the wards and the patient care and everything else. But, it's horrible, if you are in an atmosphere where you're not liked, you're not wanted; and when you first go to a ward you feel that anyway.

This student exemplified the feelings of many, in so far as her first priority on going to a new ward was not patient oriented. The students' attention, it seemed, was focused initially upon the permanent staff. They felt that it was important to get along with the trained members of staff and the auxiliaries, as well as with the ward sister. The constant movement from ward to ward demanded that the students develop a means of coping with and functioning within the system.

From the students' descriptions of these coping strategies, the notion of transiency emerges as an explanatory category, which allows some insight into the students' perception of 'just passing through' a collection of hospital wards. Transiency has advantageous and disadvantageous consequences for both students and permanent staff.

Transience as utility

One of the notable features of the students' accounts was that 'transiency' was, on the whole, accepted as a fact of a student nurse's life. This acceptance can be explained, to an extent, by the very nature of transiency. The students were willing to cope with anything during their training because it would not last longer than eight to ten weeks. The students' accounts suggest that however bad things were, and however much they disliked the work they were currently doing, the fact that it would only last a foreseeable amount of time made it bearable. The length of each ward experience was, however, important. The students needed to be in one place long enough to discover the 'unwritten rules' and the expectations of the permanent staff, to get to know the ward and its routines, and then, finally, to get to know the patients. As one student put it:

KM: How do you find that as a way of learning to become a nurse, moving every eight weeks or so?

STUDENT: As long as you are there for at least six weeks in a ward, it's not so bad, but if you are only there two weeks you haven't got time to get to know your patients or your staff, you're really a waste of time on the ward. You don't know what your patients want, don't even know if they are supposed to get up. By the time two weeks are up (. . .) you have got to learn to work with other people when you go to another hospital, when you are through your training you have to adapt again. You adapt all the way through your training.

The same student went on to describe how important her relationships with the permanent staff were.

KM: Do the permanent staff have anything to do with whether you enjoy a place or not?

STUDENT: Yes, I think they do, an awful lot. I've had no problems, but I know some of the students haven't been able to give and take. You have got to be able to give and take or you won't get anywhere in nursing. Just got to go as the wood goes.

KM: Is there an 'us and them' feeling if the students are moving through every so many weeks and there is a permanent force sitting there waiting for the next lot – do you feel?

STUDENT: Yes in some places, yes this does happen. This is why I feel you should have a rotation, sisters throughout the block [a group of wards].

KM: Do the trained staff stay quite long?

STUDENT: Yes, you have normally got, maybe two sisters, a staff nurse, two enrolled nurses and your auxiliaries are all permanent. Your students are the only ones who are floating through (. . .). Staff nurses do change quite frequently, but your auxiliaries and enrolled nurses are in with the bricks.

KM: So is it more them that you have to get along with, in some cases, than the sister?

STUDENT: Yes, in a lot of cases it's the auxiliary and enrolled nurse (. . .). Auxiliaries will come and tell you in here we do it this way, this is the way it's done. If there was a rotation the auxiliary who has been in the ward for maybe five years, would see that it is done differently on other places.

KM: And people still live?

STUDENT: People still survive, yes you know (. . .) [laughs]. Important things – there are at least one or two really permanent staff stay – they know how the doctors work. Maybe even six monthly.

KM: Is it unsettling having to go from one ward to another, or do you like the variety?

STUDENT: It's unsettling, it takes you about a fortnight to get into the routine of a new ward, you worry for about a fortnight before it.

KM: (. . .) It's almost like going to a new job every so many weeks?

STUDENT: Yes (. . .) when I know which ward I'm going to next, I go round everybody I know that's been to that ward, and find out as much as I can about it. And start worrying. Then the first week I hide away (. . .).

KM: Can you say who you do pick things up from . . .?

STUDENT: I follow the auxiliaries, because they have been there for years, know how the sister likes it done. Tend to follow them or the enrolled nurse. I've even asked domestics, because they are permanent as well, they know when sister likes her beds moved, this sort of thing.

This student advocated a rotation of staff around the wards or, in other words, that transience should be built into the system of staff allocation. This rather unusual point of view helps to clarify, albeit in an extreme way, the students' perspective on nursing, namely, a constantly changing scene. This student also felt, though, that moving around the wards was an upsetting experience. It could be that the length of stay in a ward is an important feature of transiency; a feature which makes the prevailing form of student work organization acceptable. There is, however, as she concedes, a need for some permanency. Clearly, if the main nursing workforce is to be rotated through the wards, either the style of running the wards would need to change, or some members of staff would need to remain in one place in order to initiate the itinerants in the ways of the ward. As things stand, this student's account suggests that the most stable element of the nursing workforce comprises, in the main, the nursing auxiliaries. The role of the auxiliary in the socialization of the student nurse was frequently mentioned by the students. The quotation below accurately reflects the students' experiences with this unqualified sector of the nursing workforce.

STUDENT: They [auxiliaries] have so much got into the way of doing things, that they do it a certain way and you have just got to fit in with them. That is very much so on night duty. There is no way you are going to change their routine on night duty; you just have to play along with it. You are only there for six weeks, there is not much point in stirring things up.

KM: The sort of things that you have to play along with; are they things that are really rather minor, or things that actually matter?

STUDENT: Usually very minor, for example, the ones [auxiliaries] on night duty, they are really rather good. If ever you needed anybody to use their common sense, you couldn't be better off. But it's just a bit annoying feeling that you are supposed to be in charge but you are no more in charge than fly in the air. You have the responsibility, but they just do things the way they've been doing for years. To begin with you have to rely on them, it's quite comforting at that point, it's only when you get into the way of things.

As we have seen, the students were, on the whole, prepared to accept the dominant position of the auxiliaries in running the wards. They freely admitted that the auxiliaries were of help to them both in getting to know the ward and in discovering how 'things are done here'. Also, as evidenced by the comments of the student quoted above, there was a certain amount of resigned acceptance of the status quo: 'there is no way you are going to change their routine'. In a situation where the student nurse has to subordinate her knowledge and position, such that it is, to a favoured and established routine of an unqualified member of the permanent staff, the student requires some means of rationalization. Transiency is utilized in such a situation – the student can fall back on the fact that she is 'just passing through'. As the student quoted above said 'you are only here for six weeks, there is not much point in stirring things up'. Indeed, bearing in mind the suspected collusion between auxiliaries and the ward sisters, the students were wary of adverse comment getting into their ward reports.

The auxiliaries' usefulness to the students in terms of 'on the job' teachers and a means of keeping the students 'on the right side of sister' has already been examined in chapter 1. The argument is restated here in the context of 'transiency' in order to illustrate one of the ways by which the students rationalized the transient nature of their student nurse experience. That is to say, the students were able to recognize the disadvantages of transiency, and yet rationalize its place in the training programme. The constant movement was generally accepted by the students on the grounds that moving around gave them experience, not only of different specialties, but of different ways of organizing and practising nursing. As one student put it 'I suppose it gives you a variety of ways of how to do different things'.

Students as a labour pool

One of the most important consequences of transiency seemed to be that the students provide an easily mobilized pool of labour. Student nurses are often the most obvious group to move if extra staff are required anywhere in the hospital. The students learn to adjust, fairly quickly, to the planned moves which constitute their rotation through the wards during their three-year training. Advantage of this ability to adapt is taken by the nursing managers, who are responsible for day-to-day staffing levels. The students are used as relief nurses, or as they put it 'extra pairs of hands', at very short notice. So the notion of transiency becomes relevant, in that there can be said to be 'moves within moves'. The students cannot be sure that they will be kept on the same ward, even during the span of one shift.

The following extract illustrates the point:

KM: What do you think about it as a system of training people when you look at it in those terms; you are moved around, yes, to get a look at the different things that are going on, but you're constantly breaking new ground.

STUDENT: Oh this is a good one [laughs] what I think of the system. I think it's a very good training and you learn so much, but, I really think that they *use* you as students. Well, for instance, this morning I went on at 7.30 and started cleaning in casualty, and there is a lot of cleaning to be done, so I did all that work there. At 8.30 I was moved to a heavy ward to help with bed baths and bed making, that is quite strenuous. Then at 9.00 I had to go back and start all the dressings in casualty, because it is busy there. Well, it's not common, but you find you are being used to help with the heavy work and well, it's just annoying at times, and you wonder if people do appreciate you, or whether they just think, oh, this is a student we will move her from here.

This student, having recognized that it is a 'good training', went on to say that she felt that she was being used. As she explained, student nurses could end up working a very 'heavy' day as they were invariably moved to another ward to help out over a busy period, having just worked through a busy period in their own ward. In this way the student did not experience the peaks and troughs of an average shift, but was forced to work on an atypical shift on a number of wards, and, more to the point, a shift which comprised mostly peaks.

When student nurses were used to provide short term relief in low staffed areas of the hospital, they felt that they were 'being used', or even abused. The students felt that the nurse managers viewed them as pairs of hands to be moved around the hospital at will. This phenomenon went beyond short term relief during one shift. The following extract shows how, once the students were nearing qualification, their potential as useful mobile labour was still tapped.

STUDENT: When you sit your finals you are supposed to have three choices of where you would like to go for your pre-registration. I said I would like to go to the recovery for instance and somebody said 'You'll never get recovery room' and I said, 'well, why not – that's where I'd like to go'. All your training you are pushed where you are needed as an extra pair of hands, trying to combine your clinical experience in between and oh well, they couldn't put a third-year student – 'waste of a third-year student in the recovery room' I thought – how is it a waste, that's what I'd like to do and I think I would like to do that kind of work for a while – how is it a waste, you're supposed to get a choice but in fact if you're lucky enough to choose a heavy ward, to have really liked heavy wards you'll get it sort of thing.

There's no question about it and if you asked for anything else you would probably not get it you know, and that's really terrible.

KM: So this is the time where you're supposed to have a chance to begin to learn how to run a ward and the management part of it?

STUDENT: Yes, yes, and apart from that, places you might be interested, you know, in going to [i.e. after qualified]. If it's some place heavy you choose, you would probably get it, it's a waste you see if it's of benefit to you. From a nursing management point of view, it's a waste, an extra pair of hands in the recovery room because you are only looking after one patient, one ventilator at the most. 'Come to another ward some place else, must use this girl while we've got her.'

The above extract illustrates the students' view of how they are 'used' by nursing management. The students constitute a mobile labour pool, which is used to being moved around and adapting to different wards. As they become more senior, their transient student existence is even more useful to those responsible for staff allocation. The students often stated that third-year students are seen, by the management, as a useful entity. Useful, in so far as they can be expected to take on a certain amount of responsibility or at least adapt to new work situations with little difficulty.

This point was further underlined when one student described the practice of 'making up lost time'. If students are off sick during a spell of required experience, they are expected to 'make up time' in order that the training record can be signed to the effect that the required number of hours have been spent gaining different nursing experience. This ruling was upheld when the students were off sick, but not when they missed experience due to being moved to 'help out' elsewhere.

STUDENT: And another thing that really aggrieved me – we went to do our paediatrics – a two month secondment. If you take more than three days off for something, you're sick, something like that, you've go to make up a week in paediatrics again because you've lost a week of experience. On the other hand, I spent most of my time in paediatrics helping out on the medical and geriatric wards – days here and there – was that not also losing paediatric experience?

KM: Yes.

STUDENT: You're supposed to be here but you can be used for any ward 'kids are very quiet', you know. And fair enough, I think it's terrible that there are some wards with no staff and that that's because trained staff don't want to work there. There's some wards that never keep trained staff or auxiliaries because nobody wants to work there and that's it – it's just terrible. You end up going there and yet you didn't lose out in that way; but if you took three days off, back you'd have to come. And that was much more than three days off in geriatric wards.

One of the major consequences of the transiency which characterizes the life of the student nurse is, then, a feeling of 'being used'. They felt used as a reserve supply of nurses for short term relief and for placement in unpopular areas of the hospital.

The students mentioned this abuse of the rules on loss of experience in a resigned, accepting way which belies the importance of the issue. Throughout the interviews I had the impression that the students had a lot of goodwill and positive motivation towards their work, which was difficult to dampen. The students expressed feelings of being 'used', and the question of 'making up time' is an important example of this. Such an issue might well be taken up in a militant way if a similar practice were taking place in other areas of higher education. But the students seemed to accept the 'abuses' of their position in a passive way, possibly so that they did not damage their chances of achieving registration. They concentrated on 'getting through'.

Organizational slots and stereotyped students

The students' descriptions of the attitudes of the permanent staff, in the context of a discussion of transiency, are also illuminating. The attitudes of the trained staff towards the students are affected by the fact that the majority of the nursing workforce is made up of this transient student population. The permanent staff on the wards have only a short space of time in which to get to know and assess the students who pass through their ward. The staff are unable to get to know the capabilities of each individual student on a personal basis and thus they tend to deal in stereotypes. Each ward has a number of slots labelled 'student' and individual student nurses come and go through these empty positions. Thus, each student is judged on the basis of being in the first, second, or third year and according to a generalized notion of progress through training is expected to be able to do certain things, contingent upon seniority.

Strong and Davis's (1977) discussion of role formats is helpful here. They argue that there has been a decline in the use of the concept of role. It is, they say, a concept which 'provides a link between observable behaviour and more abstract structural concerns'. Strong and Davis draw on Goffman's work, which rejects the 'deterministic notion of interaction on which traditional role theory was based'. They go on to say that, in Goffman's terms: 'the ceremonial order is based on a "working consensus" as to what the nature of social reality is to be for the present purposes, at least overtly.' Strong and Davis take this argument further in a search for more general social orders, they offer 'role formats' as a concept which encompasses both the stability in relationships and the variability which 'role' itself does not allow.

'If the norms within encounters are generated by a particular balance of resources among the participants then, where the conditions are such that this particular balance holds true across a broad range of encounters, a routinised solution is liable to emerge. Its use avoids uncertainty, cuts out initial skirmishings, avoids trouble and enables a rapid concentration on the task at hand.'

(Strong and Davis 1977)

Strong and Davis use their concept of role formats in a discussion of doctor–patient encounters. In describing role formats, they emphasize their flexibility and nature as technical solutions to interactional problems. In the context of the present study the notion of organizational slots on each ward, which awaited the permanent staff's stereotyped version of students is analytically similar. The students' behaviour can be viewed in terms of role format usage which results in the production of routinized and relatively stable responses from the variety of students on the wards.

The following student's comments make the point:

STUDENT: Yes you certainly feel that you ought to have done, say, so many catheterizations by the time you become a red stripe [i.e. third year student], because you will be sent off to do them by yourself. If you never managed to get in on the action before your third year (. . .) you feel a bit of a fool to have to say actually I've never done one before, it's never cropped up, which does happen (. . .). Or just read up your little blue nursing procedure book and you bash on regardless, which does happen, I'm sure.

KM: I wonder if there is an expectation that you should be able to do this, and you try to live up to it, by doing it, without asking.

STUDENT: I think that does happen actually.

KM: The feeling that you can't say I don't know?

STUDENT: Yes, I think it becomes more pronounced when you're a third year. One time I had to go and take out clips which I hadn't done before, as opposed to stitches which I'd taken out millions of, and I felt such a fool having to admit 'well actually I've never seen this'.

This student expressed the thoughts of many of those interviewed when she suggested that it becomes difficult, with seniority, to admit a lack of knowledge. Eventually, the 'stereotype' of the student nurse becomes something of a reality for the students themselves. They find themselves in a system which assumes that a third-year student is capable of doing certain work, and they develop a feeling that they should be able to fulfil that expectation. Moreover, the students admitted to feeling a certain amount of guilt if they could not meet the expectations of the stereotype.

The students are in a sense interchangeable in the eyes of the trained staff, that is to say, a student is not seen as an individual nurse, but rather as one student, with certain capabilities, from a pool of similar students. The trained staff use the stereotype of a student to handle this situation. The permanent staff might have Nurse Black this week and Nurse White instead next. So long as Nurse Black and Nurse White are both, say, second years and can function at the required level it matters little that Nurse White is not Nurse Black. The students' views on their treatment by the permanent staff are mixed. As it has been suggested earlier, the transient nature of the student life is rationalized by the student. They appear to accept most of what comes their way, with varying degrees of good grace, as part and parcel of the student nurse training programme. They were reluctant to openly criticize the college or the wards and, in order to make their position tenable, they would rationalize their treatment with a sense of *che sara sara*. The students were also prepared to justify the trained staff's attitude towards them. As one student put it: 'it must be very irritating for trained people as well. A new student to get into the way of things every eight to ten weeks but, at the same time, they forget you are another individual person.' This student exemplifies the views of those interviewed who, whilst not liking the trained staffs' attitudes towards students, could see that it was an understandable response to the situation, and so justified it on those grounds. We shall return to this theme later.

Settling down

The discussion of transiency and the experience of moving from ward to ward led, naturally, to the question of eventually settling down. There were varying opinions among the students concerning the desirability of staying on each ward for relatively short periods of time. The longest spell was on their first ward, where the students spent thirteen weeks; after that an average period of time on a ward was six to eight weeks. One student thought that the initial long spell on a ward was not such a good idea because she became dependent upon the ward and so her first move was 'like starting all over again'. Another student, who was indeed in the minority, was looking forward to staying in one ward for some time.

STUDENT: (. . .) the wards are very different, you go to different wards, you just have to fit in with what way the staff seem to run that ward and it's awfully difficult. I'm getting to the stage where I would like to be in a ward for a little while – six months or eight months – and just be part of that ward – not just having to go to another one, adapt to their way of thinking, just get on and . . . yes it is different in every ward.

The desire to settle in one place was, however, by no means universal, the following extract is more representative of the students' views.

KM: So are you looking forward to being able to stay in one place when qualified?

STUDENT: No [laughs] no, no because when I've done thirteen weeks in a ward, when I get to the end I think, I can't wait to see the back of this place. Not that bad, I feel after a while everything becomes (. . .) so monotonous, all you are doing is coming to work, doing your work, going home – just eating, sleeping and working. That's how it gets towards the end, 13 weeks is the longest I've had, in gynae., just same every day, doing same thing.

KM: Another example of how your three years as a student is different from what you are aiming at. Your three years as a student you do have this variety and interest and yet really what you are aiming at is being a qualified person that stays in one place (. . .).

STUDENT: True, yes. I don't think I'd like that, it worries me – well I still plan to do midwifery, I was going to do my district but I've gone off that slightly so I'll probably find sick kids[1] to do or something. I won't settle down to a staff nurse for a wee while yet. I don't like the idea of staying in one place, I think it would get very boring after a while (. . .).

KM: So you really have quite an adjustment to make once you've qualified, at that rate (. . .)?

STUDENT: Yes, I think it's because you are so used to moving around, if you had to stay in one ward for something like six months you'd be used to it (. . .) if you get bored with a ward and start not to enjoy it, think well I'm going to this next and look forward to that.

On the whole, it seems that the student nurse training provides an unrealistic introduction to nursing, because of the inherent transiency in the three-year course. One student summed up her

[1] Refers to Community Nursing training or Registered Sick Children's Nurse training.

feelings towards moving wards by saying to move was 'sometimes a relief, other times I don't want to'. She thought that it was the very fact of transiency which enabled her to enjoy some wards.

STUDENT: And I often wonder whether it's the thought that, well, I'm leaving in a fortnight, makes me begin to enjoy it a bit more. You know I've often wondered if that's the thing that has kept me enjoying it.

KM: Whereas if someone said, right you are here for two years.

STUDENT: Yes, would I be that cheery on the ward, I don't know.

KM: So how do you feel about eventually settling down somewhere?

STUDENT: Well, I'm planning to do six months, hopefully, medical, six surgical and then go on to the midwifery. So I've still got the thought of it (moving) although I've got a few months.

It seems that the students weigh the advantages against the disadvantages of settling down. The advantages they perceive have to do with getting to know a ward well and experiencing a sense of belonging. The disadvantages, however, lie in having to stay in one place and so risk boredom. The students had suggestions for ways out of this problem. There was a tendency among students to want to go on and do further certificates. This might well be a direct consequence of the unrealistically transient introduction to nursing which the students receive. By planning to go on to take further courses of training the students were projecting the notion of transiency into their post-registration period. This desire to collect further certificates can be explained, in part, by the fact that the students have been used to 'passing through' rather than 'settling down'. However, it is a complex issue which can be further explored with the aid of literature concerning what Pape (1964) has dubbed 'touristry'.

Pape looks at a group of workers who engage in 'touristry', that is: 'a form of journeying that depends upon occupation, but only in a secondary sense, in that it finances the more primary goal, travel itself.' In her study of these workers, American nurses, Pape suggests that orientation to nursing as a primary focus, in the sense of a career pattern, is by no means universal among younger nurses. She contends that older nurses are career orientated and tend to work in administration and education, whereas the younger staff nurses do not see nursing as the central part of their lives. Among the consequences of such a difference in orientation, Pape argues, is the fact that the 'tourists' use different standards in evaluating the jobs, standards which have more to do with salary, social amenities, and the potential pool of future husbands, than the professional standards which the career orientated nurses would employ. Pape was writing in the flourishing 1960s; new arguments should perhaps be included in any discussion of job opportunities in times of high unemployment.

Certainly a number of the students in the present study mentioned marriage and their plans to settle, but the data allow no more than passing comment. A suggestion offered by Dingwall and McIntosh (1978: 55), in an introduction to Pape's paper, is that the freedom of mobility which 'touristry' offers the nurse could be seen as some compensation for the lack of freedom in nursing and the restrictions of the work itself. A second point of theirs, which might have more to offer in terms of these data, is that the role of perpetual student carries with it a certain respectability.

Nursing work and student work

My research data suggest that it is possible to make a distinction between 'nursing work' and 'student work'. The central activity, patient care, is common to both forms of work: the difference lies in the time scale and location of the work.

'Nursing work' is the province of qualified staff who settle in one area and become the 'permanent staff'. 'Student work', on the other hand, is carried out in short spells of duty in a variety of wards and the distinguishing feature of its organization is its transiency. When the student has come to the end of her period of 'student work' and becomes eligible to move on to do 'nursing work' a large number prefer to continue with the 'student work' and so go on to do further courses and thus continue as student workers. There are several advantages to be gained from retaining 'student work' and its accompanying status. Qualified members of a permanent ward staff, aside from their personal responsibility for their patients, become responsible for teaching students, managing staff, and maintaining standards. Student workers, however, have a responsibility only for their own work. Because they constantly move from place to place, long-term responsibility for their actions, in terms of general policy or educational programmes, is not expected. Parallels can be drawn between the student worker and the perpetual student in academic life. Both share a carefree existence being responsible only for their own certificate collection.

Dingwall and McIntosh (1978) suggest that there might be a 'relationship between credential gathering and touristry as legitimate and illegitimate forms of mobility'. The students in this study did not mention travelling specifically in terms of 'touristry'. They talked about seeing how nursing was done in other hospitals, or undertaking a further period of training. In so far as these data go they suggest that the main reason for retaining the student role had primarily to do with the evasion of settling down. Interestingly, the students often equated settling down with a move away from the patients. This point we can now take up in terms of the students' perceptions of the role of trained staff.

Students' view of 'nursing work'

We can now take a look at the differences between the student's life and that of the permanent staff, as seen through the eyes of the students. It was apparent after a number of interviews that the students perceived that there was a difference between the activities of the three years' training to be a nurse and the essential work which a qualified nurse did. It will be recalled that student nurses are preoccupied with 'getting on with the trained staff', to such an extent that many described this as their primary aim, while patient care came second. In exploring this notion of 'getting on with the trained staff' I discovered that not only did some of the students view their relationship with the trained staff as an 'us and them' dichotomy, but they saw the staff nurse's role as one which was very different from their own. To put it at its simplest, many students felt that they spent three years doing one job in order to qualify to do another. Moreover, a number of students were not attracted to the staff nurse role because they saw it as one which was removed from the patient.

The students' preoccupation with 'getting on with the trained staff' was such that the students often measured their enjoyment of any particular experience in terms of how well they did 'get on with the permanent staff'. There were certain factors which increased the likelihood of the students getting on with the permanent staff – for instance, if the staff were prepared to allow students to feel that they were part of the ward staff, and not create an 'us and them' situation.

STUDENT: It's bad for students the fact that the same staff have been in the ward for years and years. It's very clannish, they might be very nice to you but still this three or four people who are the best of friends, been there for ages, and you are still an outsider.

KM: Who are these?

STUDENT: Trained staff, or auxiliaries as well. Usually, they are very much in with the sister, very friendly (. . .). The sister tends to go to the auxiliary rather than the student.

The student cited above described the feeling of being an 'outsider' in relation to the permanent staff on the ward. Another student described her experience in the Accident and Emergency Department which she enjoyed because, 'everybody speaks to you, there is not so much discrimination there'. She also made the point that in some areas the staff did not talk to the students unless they had to. This was also true of medical staff, 'except, of course, on night duty, when they had to speak to you because there was no one else!'

The point that this student was making had more to do with the fact that she felt accepted by the trained staff, than that they spoke to her. The transient nature of the students' placement on a ward usually meant that they were not treated as part of the ward team. This student qualified her remarks about the importance of getting on with staff. When pushed to say what it was that made a ward or department enjoyable, she said: 'The patients. It really doesn't matter if the staff are horrible, you can forget it and compensate by getting on with the other students. And, if you really hate it, well you are only there for a few weeks.'

The students were, then, aware of the problems caused by the transient nature of their role. They were in a unique position on the wards, because they were not qualified and therefore did not have the status of the trained staff; neither were they permanent staff so they were in a different position from the auxiliaries. As one student put it: 'the staff are good if they are not cliquish, which they often are. There are problems with the auxiliaries and with the trained staff; we are stuck in the middle.'

'Us and them'

'Us and them' is a rather crude way of describing the relationship between the permanent staff and the students. Nevertheless, it is a phrase which does appear to sum up the kind of divide which many of the students felt. The students described the 'cliquish' or 'clannish' relationships which often existed among the permanent staff. It was often the case that the permanent staff formed a social group, which spent off-duty time together. As it has been suggested, the ward sister knows the capabilities of her auxiliaries and is thus more likely to turn to them to 'get work done' than she is to students, who she might first have to teach what to do. This fact was mentioned by the students and, indeed by and large accepted by them, as being a reasonable way for the ward sister to proceed. One student commented: 'the staff accept you and explain things to you; in some wards it could be better. You can't expect the staff nurse to remember who has been shown what, on the whole, if you go and ask they will tell you.' This student's remarks add to the data which justify the trained staff's attitude towards students. Although the students did not like being 'outsiders' or indeed, being passed over for auxiliaries, it does seem that they had some appreciation of the difficulties which transiency presents for the trained staff. This is particularly true in the case of the ward sister. She is faced with a constant stream of students passing through her ward. Her staff nurses do not, on the whole, stay for a long period of time, which leaves the auxiliary as the stable part of her nursing workforce.

The data from this study clearly do not allow any more than speculation about the consequences of transiency for the trained staff. It is merely suggested then, that the auxiliary does not present any threat to the ward sister in terms of professional competence or desired independence; she is willing to do what the ward sister asks her to do, and hence is a reliable member of the nursing team. A ward sister who has been in one ward for a while may well find the ideas which students bring to the ward threatening, or at least disruptive. She may also find it difficult to maintain her staff nurses' loyalty should the staff nurse wish to act upon her own professional judgement and initiative. The ward sister is in a position to ride these potential hazards by using the transient nature of the students' role as a justification for dictating and controlling their behaviour, by working the opposite shifts to the staff nurse and giving her auxiliary a more prominent position than perhaps she otherwise might.

Passing out – staff nurse work

The final transition which the student has to make is that from student to staff nurse, and thus from 'student work' to 'nursing work'. It should perhaps be said that this progression is rather more complex than its linear model might suggest. The complexity is introduced by the inherent ambiguity of the student nurse's role – are they students or workers? Nevertheless, the transition has to be made, and the students had mixed feelings about it.

When I interviewed these students, there was an official provision in the training scheme for the move from student to qualified nurse; this took the form of a pre-registration period of six months, commencing after the students had taken their final examination and before they were allowed to register. It is designed to be a period of consolidation when the student should be given the opportunity to learn some of the management skills which she will require as a staff nurse. One student described her attitude towards her work if she knew that she was going to be in a senior student's or staff nurse's position on a ward: 'my approach to patients would be the same, but my approach to junior staff would have to change – I'm told I'm too pally with the junior.' I asked if she got the same results in terms of work by being 'pally' with them. 'No, I don't get the same. If you're pally they tell you they don't want to do this and that, you've got to be authoritative to a certain extent.'

One student discussed the difference between her student role and her future role as a staff nurse.

STUDENT: (. . .) You're a student and then you are suddenly
            qualified. There is a big difference. I suppose you are on
            the other side; you are making the decisions as opposed
            to acting on someone else's decisions (. . .). I'm
            dreading the responsibility.

KM: I know you have the pre-registration block eventually, but does there seem to be any kind of build up to it or is it really that you have spent three years doing one thing and suddenly, now you are it?

STUDENT: Some wards [laughs], I shouldn't say this, when you are a pre-registration student, depending on what ward you are in, you can get into the office and have a cup of tea with the staff nurses, and that sort of thing.

Students occupy a marginal position during the move from student to staff nurse. The signs that students are being accepted into the edges of the ranks of the qualified staff are substantively trivial; yet they symbolized the student's access to privileged areas of social interaction. For instance, the student above described how pre-registration nurses could get into the office for tea. Another student felt that she had crossed the barrier when she went for supper with the ward sister. Thus the students had some insights into their coming role and what it might involve. However, the transient nature of the student role had not, it seemed, prepared the students for the realities of staffing.

There was much discussion of the difference between the work of the staff nurse and that of the student. As has been said, the crucial difference was seen to lie in the move away from the patients. Although this move generally came with staff nurse status, some students argued that it began to occur when they were third-year students. The logical consequence of the trained staff moving away from patients is that it is the students who carry out the nursing care. As one student put it: 'you spend three years being told what to do, suddenly you swap roles (. . .). I've heard students say "it will be great once we are qualified, we can sit back and do the paperwork and tell the students to do everything".' The fact that the majority of the patient care is carried out by student nurses came as a surprise to a number of the students. These students had been under the impression that they would be working alongside the trained staff on the wards. This student in particular was very distressed on discovering the reality of the situation:

STUDENT: I was shocked when I came to the wards and saw all the work done by students. I think that even if you are a trained nurse you should still be able to come down and do the basic tasks, that's what I see nursing as (. . .).

I thought that the ward sister and staff nurse would muck in with you, I didn't realize that they were separate.

The student quoted above said that she did not want to become a staff nurse if it entailed leaving the patients in favour of the paperwork.

One of the notable features of the students' accounts of the staff nurses' role was the amount of potential discretion which they felt went along with it. Whilst on the one hand the students contended that the staff nurses' work entailed an inevitable move away from patients, some were adamant in their view that this need not be the case. Throughout three years of training, students had become accustomed to seeing staff nurses doing a, seemingly, different job from the one which they were currently being trained to do. Many of the students thought that the staff nurses' role need not be handled in that way, others saw no alternative, and consequently did not relish taking on that role. Those who felt that the staff nurse need not be so divorced from the patients tended to feel that she should 'pull her weight'. Our earlier discussion of 'getting the work done' illustrates this point, the main argument being that if there is work to be done, all the available staff should join in and get through it, instead of leaving the heavy work to the students. The following comment sums up the students' attitude to such discretion: 'well, I think it's really what you want to get out, if you want to back away from patients, you have got an ideal excuse.'

I pursued the question of a differentiated role for the ward sister, and to a lesser extent, for the staff nurse. The students placed more value on the fact that the ward sister 'rolled up her sleeves' and 'mucked in' than they did on her managerial activities. They suggested, for instance, that she 'must be able to join in *and* organize'. Such comments pointed to the fact that the ward sister has a separate function over and above the one shared by the rest of the nurses on the ward. One student said: 'when the staff nurse is in charge she has two roles; one working with you and one running the ward [i.e. organizing and doing the clerical work].' This student recognized the second function, which she ascribed to the staff nurse, as ward sister's work; yet if the staff nurse was 'in charge' in the absence of the ward sister it seemed that she should not, by this student's account, be allowed to relinquish her 'mucking in' role.

The students frequently referred to the 'paperwork' or 'office work' which forms part of the staff nurses' work. The 'office work' was often used to justify the move away from the direct care of patients, which the students, on the whole, saw as part and parcel of the staff nurse role. It seemed that there were, in the students' eyes, three aspects of the work of the trained staff, namely: organization of the nursing, clerical duties, and participation in direct care. The first two aspects of the work were seen to be prestigious, whereas the third was viewed more in terms of 'helping out'. The following comments illustrate the point: 'Those who have enjoyed their training want to go on with nursing care, others sit back. It depends on the ward, if it is busy the staff nurse must be out working.' And, underscoring the point about prestige:

KM: Should the ward sister join in like any other nurse?
STUDENT: Not like any other nurse, no, they have got pro-
            motion. They should get some benefits, maybe not
            benefits, maybe get out of doing the mucky jobs.

The last comment not only suggests a ranking of nursing work, but a legitimation, in terms of length of service, of a move away from the patients. It also suggests a distinction, in the minds of the students, between prestigious and lower grade 'mucky' work. This is reminiscent of Hughes's (1971) notion of 'dirty work'. The question of 'acceptable nursing work' is discussed elsewhere in the context of profession. It is mentioned here because it helps to explain why the students preferred to see the ward sister and staff nurse doing the same work as themselves. It is, to some extent, bound up with the idea that nursing work is not very desirable, and is viewed in terms of a workload to be 'got through'. It could be that the students feel that they are being left to get on with the work, while the trained staff are allowed to escape it by claiming that they have other duties to perform. If it is the case that parts of nursing work are construed as undesirable . . . 'dirty', there might be important consequences for both patient care and the development of nursing as an occupational group. The data allow us to do no more than hint at such a state of affairs in the shape of comments about the discretion attached to the staff nurse role. If newly qualified nurses are going to shun direct patient care, then it seems that there are serious questions to be addressed concerning who should do the bedside nursing. Is it to be left to the unqualified and the untrained?

If direct care is to be left to the students then they have two alternatives open to them: they can either take the same line and wait until they are staff nurses and thereby shirk the routine care, or they can redefine the staff nurse role and work with the patients. The second option would be going against the views the students hold now. Whether they would actually live up to their ideals upon becoming qualified nurses is, of course, another matter. It must be remembered that the staff nurse and ward sister roles are being discussed here as they are seen through the students' eyes. The incumbents of these roles may have a very different perspective, which might explain their behaviour in rather different terms. As it is, the students, on the whole, seemed to think that they spend three years *doing* the work in order to gain staff nurse status and, *ipso facto*, merely *supervise* the work.

Fitting in

This chapter has been concerned with the students' accounts of the frequent moves which they have to make and to which they must adjust. From their early days in training the students pass from ward to ward, and from clinical areas to college work in fairly rapid succession. This transiency, it has been argued, shapes both the students' attitude towards their work and placements, and the the permanent staff's attitude towards students. The students discussed the transient nature of their work in a very matter-of-fact way and, indeed, seemed to accept it with resignation. Not only did the students manage to rationalize the way in which they were treated by the permanent staff, they also defined the permanent staff's behaviour as a reasonable reaction to the student presence. This *tout comprendre c'est tout pardonner* attitude characterized many of the students' accounts of their difficulties both on the hospital wards and in the college of nursing.

Constant movement with no chance to settle in any one clinical area does not offer the students a realistic preparation for staff nurse work. This is yet another example of the inadequacy of anticipatory socialization in the student nurses' training experience; the students cannot get a true feel for the staff nurse role until they gain staff nurse status. The final difficulty with the system of training nurses is highlighted in the students' accounts of how they intended to avoid settling down as staff nurses. It seems that, by and large, their three years of transiency give the students an appetite for moving on rather than a yearning to settle down.

As we are coming to the end of the students' accounts of their experiences as nurses, it is perhaps worth elaborating a constant thread which has run through their story; this might best be dubbed 'fitting in'. Throughout the interviews, the students referred to the need to meet the expectations of those with whom they worked. On the hospital wards this meant, first and foremost, fitting in with the way in which a ward sister ran her ward. The other permanent staff on the wards, trained and untrained, often had different expectations which the students found they had to accommodate. The students soon discovered that to 'fit in' with the auxiliaries was not only expedient, but imperative. As we have seen, the auxiliaries were often long-standing members of the ward staff, a fact which often leads them to develop a close working relationship with the ward sister. Also, the students relied on the auxiliaries for guidance in their first few days on a new ward.

'Fitting in' constitutes a major part of the students' behaviour. First they concentrate their efforts on getting on with the ward staff, and second on the actual business of patient care. In this way, the students spend three years learning to 'pass' in both the *service* and *education* segments of nursing. The occupation by its organization and its compromise solution to the training of its recruits supports a transient approach to nursing work itself. This might be said implicitly to support a lack of commitment to nursing as an occupation. Whilst 'fitting in' and 'transience' make the present organization of nursing training sustainable, they also constitute a block to any reformulation of the curriculum. A reformulation in favour of either segment would be difficult so long as the service/education link prevails. Any impediment to curriculum changes will have implications and consequences for the occupation as a whole. These consequences, whatever they may be, merit consideration, for as Bucher and Stelling (1977:21) note: 'Segment members share a professional fate; events have similar effects on, or implications for, those in a given segment, while those same events might have quite different consequences for others in the profession.'

6

DOING NURSING AND BEING PROFESSIONAL

One of the clear themes to emerge from the students' accounts thus far is the students' belief that they learn during their training to be *students* rather than, as one might suppose, how to function as *qualified nurses*. They also developed fairly clear ideas about what they saw nursing to be. An important feature of the students' notion of nursing involves the idea that it is undoubtedly a profession. This is a widely held view among nurses and would not give rise to comment here if it were not for the fact that nursing, as the students describe it, does not fit with the conventional sociological view of a profession. On these students' accounts doing nursing work does not appear to be a professional activity. In short, the students were, on the one hand, claiming professional status for nursing, whilst on the other, describing it in workload terms, and so undercutting their claim.

The students' view of what they see nursing to be can be approached through an examination of the way in which the students described their work. The students tended to describe the work of nursing in workload terms. In fact this is the main feature of their description of nursing. Not only did they say that the work was often routine and tedious, they described it in ways which suggest that nursing is hard work to be got through by students and staff alike taking an 'all hands on deck' approach to it. There was, nevertheless, the tendency for students to talk in terms of 'profession'. It seems then, that there are links between the data concerned with what constitutes nursing and what, for the students, makes nursing a profession.

Doing nursing

The question of what is nursing is one which provokes endless debate in academic nursing circles. The interest in developing a scientific basis for nursing practice has led to a steady growth in 'models' and 'theories' and 'conceptual frameworks' in the nursing literature (cf. Schlotfeldt 1975; Orem 1971; Inman 1975; McFarlane 1976; Roy 1974 – to name but a few).

Indeed Williams (1979:89) says that: 'Identification of a conceptual framework has become a *sine qua non* for educators responsible for programs of nursing education.' It appears then that there may be a tension between those who theorize about nursing in this way and those who actually 'do nursing'.

Although the student nurses had no difficulty in talking about nursing in abstract terms, when they came to describe the different areas in which they had worked they tended to define 'nursing' in a more pragmatic way. The extract presented below serves to illustrate the ways in which the students determined what was and what was not nursing.

STUDENT: I think maybe you should get more encouragement during your time on the ward – you know, somebody saying 'you did that well' because it gives you a bit more incentive to work especially say in geriatrics and everything is more or less the same every day (. . .).

KM: Did you enjoy working in geriatrics?

STUDENT: Yes, well when I heard I was going to geriatrics I thought it's going to be a slow pace you know, because I had left surgical where you are busy all the time. But when I got there I loved it. I was a wee bit apprehensive about going.

KM: Had you been anywhere before the surgical?

STUDENT: Yes, I had been in medical before surgical (. . .). Medical is quite a fair pace and surgical is even more, but geriatrics is slower. It all depends on what's wrong with your patients [on medical ward] because if they are long-term patients you have got to do a lot more for them than if they are just waiting for Part 4 [residential care]. When they can do a lot for themselves you don't really do that much for them apart from the odd encouragement, sometimes you feel you are not doing very much for them, they are just getting on with everyday life themselves.

KM: What did you feel about that, looking at it from your point of view as a nurse, did you feel that you were nursing them (. . .)?

STUDENT: You didn't really feel that you were nursing them because I suppose you always think of nursing as the more technical sort of things like your injections and dressings and giving out medicines and things like this, but I mean, geriatrics is really just basically nursing care, you know, very basic, keeping them clean.

This student appeared to be equating fast moving, technical work with nursing; and so she did not 'really feel that you were nursing' geriatric patients. In fact, she went on to say that these older patients needed just basic nursing care. Thus, the fact that the patients were either physically independent and simply in need of encouragement, or not in need of technical care, but required only basic nursing care, made looking after these patients something other than 'real' nursing.

Such discussions suggest three main kinds of ways of talking about nursing. These were 'real nursing', which occurred mostly on surgical wards, happened at speed, and involved technical procedures or drugs administration. 'Just basic nursing care', was the term used by the students to describe the situation where the care required was exclusively nursing care, independent of medical prescription. (It is distinguished as a separate type of care because of the dismissive tone in which the phrase was often uttered.) 'Not really nursing' was the phrase more often applied to nursing in geriatric wards, or to those patients in medical wards who were elderly and in need of social care, prior to alternative arrangements being made.

Not really nursing

These three kinds of care described by the students provide the basis for the following tentative explanation of how the students came to see much of the work which they did as 'not really nursing'. The students seemed to stand in need of external reference points from which to judge whether or not their work could properly be described as nursing. The two main ones identified in the data were patient variables, notably age and severity of illness, and the location of the patient in terms of area of medical specialty.

KM: (. . .) So maybe just to start, what matters to you most in nursing, you know, when you are nursing a patient, what do you think is really probably the most important thing to you?

STUDENT: How they feel, I suppose really. It really depends on the age group you're working with. Caring for them, you do the best you can, you know, to try and understand (. . .) if it's old people, well you just want a basic nurse, you know, make sure they don't get sores and they are always clean. Because they like their pride and it gives them a wee boost and that. But really for younger people I think it's more, well, looking after them and making sure whatever's happened to them is getting sorted. But I think with younger people it's more understanding.

KM: Your understanding of them or to help them understand what's happening?

STUDENT: Both, it's sort of completely different really. You like, say a bed bath for an old person compared with a young person. Quite traumatic for the young person to have a bed bath (. . .).

KM: And how do you cope with the differences yourself? Do you have any preference for types of patients for nursing?

STUDENT: I didn't think I could ever work with old people, but I've just spent nine weeks with them and, you know, it's great.

KM: Can you say what you liked about it?

STUDENT: I think, some of them were just model patients (. . .) they really sort of help us, the ward is all they know because it was all long-term patients that were there.

KM: So what did you feel that you could do for them, as a nurse?

STUDENT: Well most of them, there was really nothing wrong with them, you know, I mean it was just like giving them an interest and, you know, even talking to them (. . .).

In contrast when asked what she liked about nursing younger people, the same student said: 'Well the only young people I've nursed were in surgical and I suppose that all the interesting operations and that, plus when you're nursing people younger, you know, in your own age group, you seem to have a lot more in common.' This student made an immediate distinction between older and younger patients when asked what she thought was important in nursing. She also made reference to the medical aspect of their care: the old people just needed a basic nurse, whereas the younger patients' care was viewed rather differently – 'make sure whatever's happened to them is getting sorted'. She found it easier to nurse the young patients because they were closer to her age group and so she felt that she had more in common with them.

The pace of the work, which related often to the nature of the condition, seemed to be an important factor for the students. It was also a factor which figures in how they determined what was and what was not 'really nursing'. The comparison of surgical and geriatric wards made by the student quoted below makes this point.

STUDENT: If you go from surgical to geriatrics then you've got problems, one extreme to another.

KM: How?

STUDENT: Surgical fast, geriatrics a very slow pace, totally different kind of nursing.

KM: What sort of things did you feel you were doing that was nursing in a geriatric setting?

STUDENT: Baths, big baths, always seemed to come back to bed bath and big bath, pressure care, oral hygiene, more occupational therapy trying to get your patients involved rather than just sitting all day.

KM: You said nursing is so different at the beginning that it's hard to sort of generalize about it. Do you feel that that was as much nursing as the work you were doing on the surgical ward was?

STUDENT: No I think on surgical you felt you were actually doing something for your patient, whereas in geriatrics you feel you are only trying to better the latter part of their life (. . .). Whereas in surgical you knew your patient would go back out, into the home environment.

KM: Is that just the age of the patient? Imagine if you were on a young chronic sick ward, constantly looking after paraplegics, multiple sclerosis – that kind of thing. How would you feel about that, day in day out, bed baths, yet they are a younger age group?

STUDENT: I think again, it would be different nursing, maybe it's just when people are old.

KM: Yes, that's what I'm trying to get at – is it because they are old, or is it because of the patient care that you are giving that makes it less like nursing?

STUDENT: I find in geriatrics it is really very difficult, I like old people, in a surgical ward then you don't mind because you have other patients (. . .) you find you can give them time and the others. But when they are all together it's hopeless, because you do something for one and they all want it, all jealous and envious of the one. Younger ones, chronic sick, multiple sclerosis, they have such a sad life in front of them, whereas old geriatrics, they've had their life, probably a good life (. . .).

KM: What would you feel towards them that you wouldn't in a geriatric ward?

STUDENT: (. . .) give more consideration to the relatives. Sometimes in geriatrics you think the family could do a lot more than they are doing, just coming at visiting, show faces for half an hour (. . .).

When the student elaborated on these differences it emerged that the pace of the work was only one factor among a much more complex set of considerations which influenced her approach to nursing and, indeed, her conception of nursing. In the surgical ward she felt that she was doing something for the patient rather than just passing the time, which she felt was the case in the geriatric ward. Doing something appeared to be an important consideration for the students. It could be argued that the students take their lead from the medical work, which is going on alongside the nursing work, and use this as their external reference for the value of their own work.

The age of the patients seems to be an important factor in determining the student nurse's attitude towards the care of them. The student quoted above at first seemed to be saying that it was the monotony of the work, all bathing, which made the work in the geriatric ward both difficult to do and difficult to regard as nursing. Yet when I asked about the young chronic sick, the student shifted her argument and explained her attitude in terms of the patient's age rather than the care required. She was, however, prepared to concede that nursing old people in a setting where there were also younger patients was different from geriatric nursing, because she thought that nurses could then devote the necessary time to old people when there were not too many competing with one another for the nurses' time. This comment shifts the focus of the argument back to the heaviness of the work rather than the simple fact of the patient's age.

Alternatively, the actual setting in which the patients were nursed could be said to have some bearing upon how the nurses view the work there. Old people in surgical wards are candidates for 'real nursing' because they have a condition which nurses recognize, because they take the medical lead, as legitimate. Similarly, care of the young chronic sick, which to all intents and purposes resembles care given to old people, merits the term 'real nursing' because of the way in which students view the young patients. The student (above) said that the old person has had their life whereas the young chronic sick have a sad life. This led her to view the nursing of each group in a different way. Indeed, a moral judgement entered into the student nurse's justification for having a more favourable attitude towards nursing the young chronic sick than the elderly. The nursing actions were the same but the social context different; this caused the student to deem the younger patient to be more worthy of 'real nursing' than the elderly patient.

The reasoning underlying the students' classification of their work as 'nursing' or 'not really nursing' varies according to circumstances, social and situational. The situational argument is interesting in the light of the findings of Baker (1978) in relation to the care of geriatric patients. Baker coined the term 'honorary geriatric' to describe patients who: 'because their nursing care was indistinguishable from that received by patients whom the nurses defined as "geriatric" and who conformed to the geriatric stereotype in every particular except age' (p. 247). Baker describes the care of patients of different ages within a geriatric setting. The nurses in Baker's study were, seemingly, able to move beyond the situational dictates of a geriatric setting in the care of some patients. Baker cites one patient who, although in her eighties, was treated preferentially, and in a way which was not in the 'routine geriatric style'; this was because she had the status of a 'young patient'. She had lived for many years on the ward, after being admitted as a younger patient, and her original status had remained with her. The student in my study appeared to require the older patients to be 'diluted' with younger ones, and indeed transferred to the younger setting of the surgical ward before the 'geriatric stigma' and the 'not really nursing' labels could be removed. Baker suggests that in defining 'geriatric' we must distinguish formal meaning from subjective meaning. A formal definition includes all the patients on the wards designated 'geriatric'; whereas the subjective meaning of 'geriatric' derives from nurses' categorizaation of particular patients as 'geriatric' on the basis of their possessing certain, usually discreditable, attributes.

Most of the items of data, which lead to the formulation of the 'real nursing'/'not really nursing' distinction, were concerned with the comparison between work on geriatric wards and the more acute wards. These comparisons were made by the students in terms of doing something for the patient, or seeing rewards in terms of cure and discharge home. This concept of nursing is exemplified by one student who thought that patients should actually 'look ill'.

STUDENT: When I did my geriatrics I didn't find it stimulating at all, I enjoyed it but I found that the patients never got a lot to do, just sat there (. . .). There were no activities to do for them, there was music and things like that but it was up to the students to make something happen that day. But you always felt when I leave here nothing is going to happen, it's just going to go back into the same old routine because the auxiliaries that have been there for 25 years, run the ward their way (. . .). I didn't mind it but I didn't think it was nursing as such.

KM: Could you say what you think nursing as such is, what has to go into it that makes it nursing?

STUDENT: I don't know if you expect somebody to be ill, you know, look ill, for it to be nursing. A lot of the old people, they are not actually ill, they are there because they are a danger to themselves in the community. Maybe it's just that they are not ill and they don't, maybe, need so much from you, it was more supervisory than anything else. I don't know, maybe it was just lack of physical care that you had to give (. . .).

This student also makes the point that she did not feel needed in the situation where the work did not constitute 'nursing as such'. This is perhaps not too surprising because nurses, as conventional wisdom has it, commonly make patients dependent upon them and therefore feel somewhat impotent when they find themselves in a situation where the patient requires little of them.

So far, then, the data have suggested that the students preferred the technical aspects of their work and had a tendency to describe such work as 'really nursing'. Criteria used in the process of labelling work as 'not really nursing' or 'real nursing', it has been suggested, have for the most part to do with the location of the patient and various patient attributes. However, the data also suggest that the student nurses take their lead from the medical profession in determining which areas of care they are most prepared to value and consequently refer to as 'real nursing'. We can now turn our attention to this medical influence.

Medical dominance

Whilst it must be said that this was not always the case, the students required some medical or technical overlay in their work before they were prepared to categorize care as 'real nursing'. 'Basic nursing care' was often described in terms of 'anyone can do it' and thus dismissed as '*just* basic nursing care'. One student put a rather different view. Although this was the only one of this kind, it is worth noting before the discussion progresses, if only to point up the fact that there is scope for differences of opinion. Asked what she thought constituted the nursing part of geriatrics, she described their 'social care' and said: 'keeping them occupied is nursing because they are in hospital to be nursed, and they require amusement so that is your job in that kind of work (. . .) whatever the patient requires is nursing.' This response represents a rather extreme nominalist approach to nursing, whereby whatever the nurse did became nursing.

Preference for technical, medically oriented work was evidenced by students favouring surgical wards.

KM: Have you any preference yet between medical and surgical?

STUDENT: Surgical. I don't like medical, it's too slow and patients are around for maybe months on end. In surgical you get a different side of it, the turnover of patients is a lot quicker than it is on the medical side; plus you see a lot more different things coming in (. . .).

KM: Is it the speed you like, or the variety?

STUDENT: I think it's both, actually. I like the speed of the work
           and the variety of work. You're never just sitting
           nursing chest infections and MIs [coronaries] which is
           all it seems to be down medical, or diabetics with
           undiagnosed diabetes coming in or diabetics coming in
           with infections (. . .).

KM: (. . .) Do you find that you nurse in the same way in
           medical and surgical?

STUDENT: No, I've found it's different, totally different.

KM: What sorts of things are different?

STUDENT: Up in surgical you have a got a lot more observations
           to do on the patients than what you have on medical.
           On surgical I feel I got more responsibility.

Another student when asked whether she had preferences in
nursing said:

STUDENT: I like surgical rather than medical.

KM: Why?

STUDENT: Surgical is better than medical. Quicker turnover of
           patients, it's faster.

KM: Is that just the day-to-day pace?

STUDENT: Yes, although medical care is just as fast in a different
           way. Treatments are faster in surgery, medical in-
           vestigation takes a long time.

KM: Seeing results you mean?

STUDENT: Mm, medical nursing could be good if you are there a
           long time so you could see results, but for us only there
           eight weeks, a lot of patients you don't see go
           through (. . .).

Some students preferred surgical wards, not only because of the
pace of the work, but because of the results which are, generally
speaking, more forthcoming than they are on medical wards. This
preference is interesting, for one might argue that in the areas
where the doctors are playing the 'sit and wait' game, as is often the
case in the medical wards, there is more in the way of independent
nursing care to be given. Whereas in the surgical wards, the bulk of
the work is either done by the surgeons or is dictated by them,
consequently there is little scope for nursing which is independent
of medical directives.

Freidson's (1970b:141) discussion of medical dominance is relevant here; it is a theme which is taken up again later. Freidson argues that:

'In the medical organisation the medical profession is dominant. This means that all the work done by other occupations and related to the service of the patient is subject to the order of the physician. The profession alone is held competent to diagnose illness, treat or direct the treatment of illness and evaluate the service. Without medical authorisation little can be done for the patient by paraprofessional workers.'

If we accept Freidson's position, then it should perhaps be of little surprise that the student nurses look to medicine as a legitimating body, when they want to determine which aspects of their work should be valued. Freidson (1970b:144–45) suggests that the division of labour in the health services, which is organized around the professional dominance of medicine, produces a social order similar to that provided by a bureaucratic division of labour. Thus he says:

'The paraprofessional worker is, then, like the industrial worker, subordinated to the authority of others. He is not, however, subordinated solely to the authority of bureaucratic office, but also to the putatively superior knowledge and judgement of professional experts.'

This professional dominance argument, which Freidson uses in order to describe the relationship between medicine and other health care workers, including nurses, might be used to explain the student nurses' tendency to value medically dominated aspects of their work. The students were prepared to call the technical and largely medically prescribed aspects of their work 'real nursing' and to dismiss as 'not really nursing' those parts of their work which are not dependent upon medicine. It seems that the students in this study were reflecting, in their attitudes, the hierarchy of specialties in medicine (see Shortell 1974). These data allow no more than speculation. The relationship between the preferred clinical areas of nurses and the distribution of merit awards in medicine might repay further investigation.

If the current move towards nursing developing an independent body of knowledge, couched in nursing models and theories, is in tune with the nursing work done on the wards, one would expect there to be a heightened interest in the areas which allowed scope for such developments in nursing rather than the medically dominated areas. Two possible explanations for this not, apparently, being the case are offered here on the basis of these data. These explanations are bound up with the students tendency to dismiss the work described as 'just basic nursing care'. If the nursing care, which is potentially independent of medicine, is seen in terms of 'anyone could do this', it does not appeal to nurses because it is either low status work or not sufficiently interesting work. The remedy for both of these difficulties with nursing work is to be found in medicine. The students take their kudos from medically dominated work and maintain an interest in their work by introducing a theoretical element, pertaining to medicine. The question of the introduction of 'theory' to the student nurses' programme in order to sustain their interest in nursing has already been discussed. The following extracts illustrate the point for the purposes of the present discussion.

KM: You talked about being an extra pair of hands and we were just talking about what makes nursing nursing. Other students I've spoken to have talked about working in geriatric wards and just keeping the patients amused, get them out of bed and put them back to bed again and they say that's not really nursing. Do you find that what you do in different wards you could either say was nursing or was not nursing?

STUDENT: Yes, well to a point yes, everything is nursing to me, in my depressed moments, I'm just going to leave – I've got to be Jack of all trades and master of none (. . .). I mean things like, I mean some geriatric wards, in a way it's nursing at its essence, you're doing everything for that patient (. . .). But the patient knows he's got a family, they will go back and assume a normal existence. In a long-term geriatric ward there's nothing, you have got to think everything for them, that is probably nursing at its best where you do everything for them, on the other hand you can get so unstimulated because you are getting nothing back, no results. Really it is a constant toil, really and no results and in a way it's nursing, but it's not nursing. On the other hand, some of the work done in geriatric wards anybody could do it – you don't really need a very expert person but you could use it to the patient's benefit if you were really interested enough to know.

These comments demonstrate the tension which exists for the students: geriatric nursing is seen simultaneously as something which can be done by anyone and as an activity which, if carried out by an expert, could benefit the patients. Typically it was the lack of reward or results and the tedium which caused the students to dislike geriatric nursing, or at least, to dismiss it as 'not really nursing'.

The student cited below found her rewards in the orderly way in which surgical wards proceeded:

STUDENT: There is a lot of order, you get your patient coming in, your ordinary admission for appendix or something, not an emergency, then you see them getting from really down after the operation to fine; whereas in medical wards patients come in with, say, hypertension, you can't do much for them. Doctors do blood tests, you the drug therapy, we administer the drugs, fair enough, but as far as you are concerned they are virtually the same as when they came in. You find the medical wards get bunged up with stroke patients. I'm working in a medical ward at the moment, half of it is all stroke patients, that need everything done – which I suppose you could say is just like geriatrics. The other side is acute, it doesn't mix well, there is not enough staff to manage the two different aspects of it (. . .).

Similarly, another student preferred surgery because she thought it was more interesting.

STUDENT: You are on the go all the time and it is interesting, knowing all about drips and drains and types of operations, I was very junior when I first did surgical, I didn't really get told much, just sort of left to get on, making beds and washing folk and that, but now (. . .) you are told a bit more about the condition of the patients and this is really interesting; also types of operations.

These extracts illustrate the reliance on medicine to provide, for nursing, both interest and work of a higher status than 'just basic nursing'. The stroke patients, whom the student says 'bung up' the medical wards, arguably have needs which could be met by nursing actions which are not dependent upon medical prescription. Yet, these patients do not appear to be popular with the students. They prefer patients who, by virtue of their medical condition, afford more in the way of visible results and hence some kind of reward in exchange for the time nurses invest in them. It seemed not to matter whether these results stemmed from nursing actions, the mere fact that there were evident results was sufficient reward for the student nurses. The nursing work on the surgical ward was seen to be closely associated with the doctors' work which produced the ready and visible improvement. Also, interest in the students' work was provided by the possibility of learning about the operations and 'all about the drips and drains'. Such technicalities, it can be argued, are a means of sustaining the student's interest in the tedium of the routine work of a surgical ward.

The nursing literature concerned with nursing functions which are independent of the doctor is growing. The move by a small, influential minority towards making nursing an academically respectable discipline is gaining strength. Yet, according to the students, ultimately much of the patient care, however it is planned, using any number of theories and care plans, is routine and, at times, tedious. As one student put it: 'However far you go into the technical side of nursing you can't get away from basic nursing care. There is now much more theory that somebody on the ward must know, but you will always need nurses to do the basics.' This apparent dichotomy led the investigation of the students' ideas in relation to the status of their work. It seems that 'just basic nursing care' is both the core of nursing and yet so easily dismissed in favour of a 'higher status work'. We shall now turn to the students' accounts of their work, in terms of their relation to the notion of 'profession'.

A note on 'profession'

Carr-Saunders and Wilson (1933), in their seminal work, surveyed a number of professions and thereby sought to describe the emergence of professions, the rise of professional association, and

the effects of state intervention and regulation upon the organization of the professions. There has been an abiding interest in the
sociology of professions, with work focusing on professionalization, professionals within bureaucratic organizations, and the
power of professions. (See Etzioni 1969; Vollmer and Mills 1966;
Scott 1969; Abrahamson 1967; Hall 1968; Freidson 1970a and
1970b; Johnson 1972.)

The main concern of much of the work on professions has been
to answer the question 'What is a profession?' although this was
never the explicit aim of Carr-Saunders and Wilson (1933: 3) who
state that:

> 'It is no part of our purpose to attempt to draw a line between
> professions and other vocations, we are not concerned to say
> what vocations are professions and what are not. . . . Indeed,
> the drawing of a boundary-line would be an arbitrary pro-
> cedure, and we shall not offer either now or later, a definition of
> professionalism. Nevertheless, when we have completed our
> survey it will emerge that the typical profession exhibits a
> complex of characteristics, and that other vocations approach
> this condition, more or less closely, owing to the possession of
> some of these characteristics, fully or partially developed.'

Carr-Saunders and Wilson, whilst denying the production of a
definition of 'professionalism', do come close to it with their
'complex of characteristics'. In adopting this approach to the
analysis of profession they could be said to foreshadow the work of
the attribute theorists. This has been the dominant approach to the
study of professions. The attribute theorists' analysis assumes that a
set of criteria can be identified and used in order to determine
whether or not an occupation is a profession. These criteria have
proved to be difficult to draw up; Millerson (1964: 5) has produced
perhaps the most rigorous list. Drawing on the work of others in
the field, he produces a league table of professional criteria. He also
offers a definition:

> '[Profession] is a type of higher-grade, non-manual occupation,
> with both subjectively and objectively recognised occupational
> status, possessing a well-defined area of study or concern, and
> providing a definite service, after advanced training and
> education.'
>
> (Millerson 1964: 10)

This definition does not take us very far along the way to knowing what is meant when someone uses the term 'profession'. Particularly problematic is Millerson's use of the phrase 'subjectively and objectively recognised occupational status'. In an attempt to provide some basis for understanding the usage of 'profession', this discussion will focus on the work of Freidson (1970a and 1970b) and Becker (1962).

Freidson (1970a) provides a different leverage on profession from that offered by the attribute theorists. His analysis of the medical profession is drawn upon here. He sets out to present:

> 'an extended analysis of a profession . . . emphasis is on both sides of the meaning of the word "profession" as a special kind of occupation, and "profession" as an occupation which has assumed a dominant position in the division of labour, so that it gains control over the determination of the substance of its own work. Unlike most occupations it is autonomous or self directing. The occupation sustains this special status by its persuasive profession of the extraordinary trustworthiness of its members. The trustworthiness it professes naturally included ethicality and knowledgeable skill.'
>
> (Freidson 1970a: xvii)

Freidson makes a distinction between 'professionalism', which he described in terms of an ideology of profession, based upon a set of attributes said to be characteristic of professionals, and 'profession' which he defines in terms of structural distinctions. Professionalism, he says, seems able to exist independently of professional status.

Freidson's (1970a: 82) major criterion for making professions distinct from other occupations is that they must have a position of legitimate control over work. This is clearly not the case with nursing which comes into the class of occupations which Etzioni (1969: v) has called the 'semi-professions'. These he describes as:

> 'a group of new professions whose claim to the status of doctors and lawyers is neither fully established nor fully desired. Lacking a better term we shall refer to those professions as semi-professions. Their training is shorter, their status less legitimated, their right to privileged communication is less established, there is less autonomy from supervision or societal control than "the" professions.'

Freidson's main thesis is that the consequences of the paramedical occupations being organized around the central established profession of medicine, are that, whilst they lack autonomy, responsibility, authority, and prestige, they do possess elements of professionalism. He sums up the nurses' dilemma thus.

> 'while nursing originally established itself as a fully-fledged occupation of some dignity by tying itself to the coat-tails of medicine, it has come to be greatly concerned with finding a new, independent position in the division of labour. One of its dilemmas, however, lies in the fact that its work can no longer be controlled by the occupation itself. Most nursing takes place inside the hospital where nursing has not achieved autonomy.'
>
> (Freidson 1970a:63)

For Freidson, 'professionalism' is the means by which:

> 'subordinate occupations claim to the public and to themselves that they have worthy tasks of service and evidence personal qualities of professionals . . . indeed the claim is to be a profession as such, if only by identification with the profession of medicine.'
>
> (Freidson 1970a:67)

It can be argued that Freidson's analysis is not all that different from the attribute theorists' work. For example, Dingwall (1977:119) argues that Freidson, having found his 'fundamental criterion' in professional autonomy, uses it in his identification of other 'professions' in the same vein as the attribute theorists.

> 'There is a central ambiguity in his [Freidson's] work between specifying an objective definition of "profession" and examining the subjective knowledge of collectivity members. . . . The strain between the objective and subjective elements is usually resolved in favour of the objective. This, of course, leads Freidson into legislating a social reality in just the same way as a classic attribute theorist.'
>
> (Dingwall 1977:119–20)

Becker's (1962) paper concerned with the nature of profession is discussed here as he cites Flexner's (1915) classic paper 'Is social work a profession?' in order to demonstrate the attribute approach to the study of professions. Flexner, he says, set forth six criteria for distinguishing professions from other kinds of work:

'professional activity was classically *intellectual*, carrying with it great personal responsibility; it was *learned*, being based on great knowledge and not merely routine; it was *practical*, rather than academic or theoretic; its *technique* could be taught, this being the basis of professional education; it was strongly *organised* internally; and it was motivated by *altruism*, the professionals viewing themselves as working for some aspect of the good of society.'

(Becker 1962: 88)

On testing out his criteria against the attributes of certain occupations, Flexner found that social work had no technique of its own and thus was not a profession.

He then qualified his objective criteria drastically with the caveat:

'what matters most is professional spirit. All activities may be prosecuted in the general professional spirit. In so far as accepted professions are prosecuted at the mercenary or selfish level, law and medicine are ethically no better than trades. In so far as trades are honestly carried on, they tend to rise toward the professional level. . . . The unselfish devotion of those who have chosen to give themselves to making the world a fitter place to live in can fill social work with the professional spirit and thus to some extent lift it above all the distinctions which I have been at such pains to make.'

(Becker 1962: 88)

This caveat, in a sense, undermines Flexner's whole analysis; for it suggests that a profession is only a profession in so far as some sociologist is prepared to say it is. Becker (1962: 89–92) suggests that the difficulties experienced among students of profession in trying to arrive at an agreed-upon usage of the term 'profession' stems from the fact that: 'one term is being made to do two quite different jobs.'

The term 'profession' is used by social scientists as a scientific concept, in order that they might distinguish professions as one of several forms of occupational organization in a society. Yet, Becker points out that 'profession' is not a term used solely by social scientists.

'Laymen habitually use it to refer to certain kinds of work and not to others, which they describe variously by "business",

"sciences", "trades", "rackets" and the like. Used in this way in
the ordinary intercourse of our society, the term has another
kind of meaning. Instead of describing and pointing to an
abstract classification of kinds of work, it portrays a morally
desirable kind of work. Instead of resembling a biologist's
conception of a mammal, it more nearly resembles a
philosopher's or theologian's conception of a good man.'

(Becker 1962:89)

Becker suggests that there is nothing wrong with using the term in
both senses, that is to 'use morally evaluative criteria to create an
objectively discriminable class of phenomena'. Yet, he says,
difficulties arise because people conventionally apply profession, in
a morally evaluative sense, to certain occupations, typically
medicine and the law. Similarly, convention refuses to allow the
use of the term profession for certain occupations (Flexner uses
plumbing as an example). Nevertheless Becker says: 'to some
people, both those within the professions in question and laymen,
it is not so clear that medicine and law are necessarily morally
praiseworthy and plumbing is not' (Becker 1962:91). The problems surrounding the use of the term 'profession' exemplify what
Becker says is a perennial problem in social sciences, when the
discipline's concepts refer to matters which concern both the
people they are applied to and the general public.

'In an effort to make concepts abstract and scientific, we tend to
lose touch with the conceptions of laymen. Yet, if we try to
incorporate their concerns into our concepts, we are faced with
ambiguities like those surrounding profession.'

(Becker 1962:91)

Becker offers a way out of this difficulty and proposes that we
should give up the attempt to produce a definition which is
objectively specific whilst still conveying the layman's sense of
which occupations are really professions. Instead, he says we should
take a radically sociological view, regarding professions simply as
those occupations which have been fortunate enough, in the
politics of today's work world, to gain and maintain possession of
that honorific title. In this way 'profession' is not used as a scientific
concept but as a 'folk concept', that is as part of the apparatus of the
society we study, to be understood in the way that society uses it.
Becker goes on to look at what he calls the characteristics of the

'honorific symbol'. This analysis, he says, is different from the attribute theorist approach; because where they look at characteristics of *existing* occupational organizations, Becker is concerned with 'conventional beliefs about what those characteristics *ought* to be'. He argues that:

'Although people disagree as to what occupations are "really" professional . . . beneath these surface disagreements we can find substantial agreement on a set of interconnected characteristics which symbolize a morally praiseworthy kind of occupational organisation.'

(Becker 1962:93)

In order to effect this analysis of the 'symbol' Becker draws on the work of the attribute theorists on the grounds that these definitions tried to take account of popular conceptions and 'furnish an adequate source of characteristics out of which to construct the symbol of profession in our society'. He concludes that 'symbol' does not describe any actual occupation but rather, it is 'a symbol that people in our society use in thinking about occupations, a standard to which they compare occupations in deciding their moral worth'. Becker recognizes the limitations of symbols, particularly that they might become so removed from reality that they are unattainable.

Dingwall (1976) suggests that sociologists should seek to understand the 'practical usage' of 'profession', rather than attempt to legislate a correct use of the term. He set out to examine health visitors' use of 'profession' in relation to their own and others' behaviour in terms of 'professional' and 'non-professional' conduct. In this endeavour Dingwall drew up a summary of his field data in a schematic form. The resulting list included summary statements concerning the health visitor as a person, the autonomy of health visiting work, the attributes of the occupation, responsibilities for supervising others' work, equality of health visitors with other professionals, the discrete area of work of health visiting, and the health visitor's assumption that her view of her social location was accepted by others. The formal scheme drawn up from the data is not definitive or exhaustive but Dingwall (1977:122–23) claims that:

'Nevertheless by looking at the usage of terms over a series of interactions we may seek to assemble a repertoire which might

plausibly correspond to some more or less organised interpretive scheme held by members of the health visiting community.'

This analysis, Dingwall says: 'involved abandoning any attempt to
legislate the definition of a "profession" and, instead, the study of
its usage to establish the activities of health visitors as a "profession" rather than an "occupation".' He concludes that:

> 'health visitors' claims to professional status are based upon their
> conceptions of the social structure of their society and the
> relative placing of occupations within it. This involves the
> location of health visiting as equal, inferior or superior to other
> occupations. Such self location is not, of course, necessarily
> recognised by those other occupations.'
>
> (Dingwall 1977: 141)

Dingwall's discussion of health visitors' claims to professional
status is helpful in considering these data.

Students' usage of 'profession'

Following Dingwall, I looked for opportunities to explore the
students' use of the term 'profession'. During the course of the
fieldwork, I gained the impression that the students used the term
in an everyday sense, taking it for granted that nursing is a
profession. In studying the transcripts, it appeared that the students
used the actual word sparingly yet somehow managed to invoke
the concept 'profession' in order to set nursing aside from 'just
another job', or indeed, from the work of the nursing auxiliaries.

The students' limited usage of the term 'profession' presents an
interesting question for analysis. The kinds of things the students
were saying appear to amount to notions which sociologists would
combine and label as a claim to profession; yet the students did not
actually articulate this claim.

Despite the fact that the students were apt to describe their work
as 'not really nursing' – and, implicitly, if in no other way, to
suggest that a lot of nursing work required little specialized skill, let
alone knowledge – they nonetheless termed it 'professional'. Again
it should be borne in mind that the students used the word in
different senses, few in the tradition of Carr-Saunders and
subsequent exponents of 'profession'.

The following extracts illustrate the students' understanding of
their work:

KM: Are you conscious of needing the exam at the end of the day? Of needing to pass it? Is it there all the time, the pressure?

STUDENT: At the moment, yes. [The student was in college at the time.]

KM: Do you feel it in the college more than on the wards?

STUDENT: Yes, yes but I don't think it's a bad thing, I think it would sort of sift out the ones that, I wouldn't want myself to be associated with, I think (. . .).

KM: Sorry, how do you mean?

STUDENT: Well, I think, if you can't get through the exams, I think they have got to keep a certain standard in nursing. Even things like headlines in the papers 'nurse found with several men' (. . .) it annoys me, it maybe sounds snobby but, it turns out to be an auxiliary or something. We are all classified as 'nurse'. We're not all, we are all nurses but there are definitely different categories.

KM: It's a difficult argument in some areas.

STUDENT: Yes it is, but I think there have to be certain standards and people have to step in line with those, otherwise we are all going to go down with them (. . .). You know, sort of a poor standard of nursing in a hospital, everybody is going to be classed as the same, so I do think the exams are essential.

This student does not once use the word 'profession'. Nevertheless she is making a claim for the separate categorization of the occupational group. Indeed her comment about sifting out those with whom she would not want to be associated suggests that although she does not use the term 'profession' she has in mind some judgemental yardstick, akin to Becker's 'symbol'. Her remarks suggest that she would reserve the term 'nurse' for a group of workers who might do the same work as nursing auxiliaries but who are also in some sense different. This position was taken by several of the students. Whilst they could not always say why nursing either deserved a particular position in the classification of occupations, or was indeed, a profession, they displayed a tendency to want to set it apart as a rather special occupation.

The student's comments below illustrate the inability to define profession.

KM: (. . .) I don't know if you feel that it is more of a profession than a job?

STUDENT: A profession.

KM: What makes it that?

STUDENT: It's not just a job. You don't just go in and do it, it progresses. A job you just go in and do, come back and leave it. A profession you progress in, I can't explain it.

Students' accounts of their work varied. Some chose to discuss nursing in relation to occupational alternatives, as evidenced by the following extracts:

KM: (. . .) so in general terms, can you say what you think is important in nursing?

STUDENT: Depends what you want out of it I think.

KM: You mean personally, can you perhaps say why you came into nursing?

STUDENT: I've been working with people before in a public relations department, highways department, shops on Saturdays before I started nursing. I fancied working with people, I couldn't bear to be shut in an office all day, just didn't appeal to me at all, boring. So either nursing or teaching, I did decide when I was doing my 'O' grades; the careers mistress informed me that there weren't many jobs going but there were opportunities to go into nursing in various parts of the country, so I decided to do nursing.

KM: How have you found it since you started, what do you like about it?

STUDENT: I like working in the wards but I didn't realize that there would be so many exams and things (. . .).

Similar views were expressed by another student:

KM: (. . .) What do you really think is important in nursing?

STUDENT: I think you have got to have a liking for people, working with people, got to have a compassion towards people. I think nursing will have to put out a lot more advantages of coming into nursing in the future; as far as I have seen on the wards they are really short staffed.

KM: What brought you into nursing?

STUDENT: I wanted a job where I could work with people and I wanted to get away from home, that's maybe my main reason, and nursing just seemed to be a job which suited me, but I've found out to my cost it isn't the job that suits me.

KM: Can you elaborate on that?

STUDENT: Well for one thing, coming away from home I find I can't live on the salary, I'm overdrawn every month, I think that is just coming away from home. And you are given more responsibility on the wards than I think you can cope with and I don't like working shifts.

The students cited above discussed their reasons for 'doing nursing' in terms of the attractions of the work in contrast with other possible occupations. Social and structural considerations, which had to do with conditions of work and the lifestyle which could be achieved through the work informed these students' views of nursing.

KM: You said at the beginning that the thing that you thought was most important was caring for your patient and caring for your profession. Do you see nursing as a profession – how do you view nursing?

STUDENT: Oh yes I definitely see it as a profession. And I think if we are going to have any advancement – there have been so many advances in medicine that nursing has obviously got to follow – and if we don't start banding together and sticking up for ourselves as a profession I think we are going to lose all status. As it is I don't quite know what our status is within the general public, how they feel about us. I'm sure the almost condescending way they say 'oh you do such a wonderful job', really they mean, 'I don't really know how you can do it, it is so horrible, but we need someone to do it so you must be wonderful'; that comes out in a lot of people's attitudes. It's a very middle-class profession, so many people become student nurses and they are always fairly well educated, not just a lot of people who have got a couple of 'O' grades, they have managed to go on

and do 'Highers',[1] and quite a few of them have even
been to university and colleges and then decided to go
back to nursing because they have decided that they
don't want a more 'classical' type of education, but
want to be doing things with people. Nursing seems to
be a middle course for most of them, they like to have
responsibility, and at the same time be looking after
people. In that way nursing is good (. . .).

In the first two extracts above the students were talking about
nursing in terms of job expectations and job satisfaction. The desire
to work with people, not surprisingly, cropped up in most
students' accounts of why they chose nursing. The student in the
last extract defended the status of nursing work. She saw nursing as
a profession for the educated middle classes who want a responsible
job working with people, but do not want a university type
education. She stressed the point that many student nurses are
eligible for university entrance. This comment stands in rather
sharp distinction from that made by the student who was surprised
to find that nursing was 'so academic'. The same student went on
to discuss the work of auxiliaries. She felt that there should be
more qualified staff actually doing the nursing care.

KM: (. . .) that doesn't quite square does it with what we
talked about earlier, about how nurses say that they
want to work with and help people. Now we are talking about they want to move away from patients (. . .).

STUDENT: Yes, if you really wanted to work with people you
would be an auxiliary because they are the ones that
always work with people, they never progress so they
are always with the patients. That's why perhaps
nursing should perhaps be changing more, there
should be less auxiliaries about – and I'm always
changing my mind about what should be done – but in
some way there should be more trained staff and less
auxiliaries, so that there are more trained people
looking after and doing the basic care for the patients,
and always doing the baths and bed baths.

[1] 'Highers' are the Scottish education system's near equivalent to 'A'
levels.

KM: Yes, because the picture that you are painting suggests
           that the students do that [i.e. basic care], and if there are
           trained staff there and students, the staff are happy to
           say 'oh well, the students should do that because they
           are here'.

STUDENT: Yes, and some of the trained staff they even prefer to be
           doing things like just making empty beds, rather than
           doing basic things like beds and bed baths; which is so
           wrong, because you always learn so much about the
           patient in intimate surroundings, you just get to know
           them so well (. . .). Maybe it is a time we got back to
           basic, more basic nursing.

KM: Raise the status of it, I wonder if that is at the root of it;
           a drug trolley is high status, washing somebody is not
           so good.

STUDENT: [Heavy with sarcasm] Yes, anybody can do that,
           whereas only trained staff or two students can do the
           drugs (. . .). I think things are a bit upside-down.

She went on to say that senior student nurses displayed the
tendency to move away from the patients even before they joined
the ranks of the trained staff. They preferred to do the more
technical work and to leave the basic nursing to the up and coming
juniors. This point recurred throughout the study.

I pursued the question of the students' urge to move away from
the patient, by asking how far the students thought that this desire
was in keeping with the 'professional' ethos, or even the claim to
want to 'work with people'. In the extract quoted above the
student thought that 'things were beginning to get a bit upside-
down'. By this she meant that nursing was being done, in the main,
by untrained nursing auxiliaries and students, instead of by
qualified staff. In other words if students come into training in
order to nurse patients when they qualify, why is it that they
appear to move away from direct patient care as they approach
qualified nurse status?

The students are faced with a problem when they consider the
nature of their work. The student cited above exemplifies the
tension which exists, when she tentatively suggests that there
should perhaps be less auxiliaries. It seems, then, that in making
claims to 'profession', if indeed they are, the students are left with a
dilemma. If they declare that nursing is a profession, which

requires training, and has a body of skills and knowledge, they must reach the conclusion that untrained auxiliaries should not practise nursing. On the other hand, since auxiliaries do engage in very similar work to that undertaken by many students, they might equally well argue that if auxiliaries can do nursing it is not specialized work and therefore cannot be considered to be a profession. Johnson (in Hardie and Hockey 1978:115) supports this second view, in a paper concerned with 'nursing professionalization'.

> 'Perhaps the greatest stumbling block to professional elevation is the vast range of work which goes on under the nursing rubric. Nursing auxiliaries are not only numerous, they carry out work of an undeniably important kind with little or no training.'

This dilemma raises the original questions posed by Becker (1962) surrounding what is meant by 'profession'. We shall return to this question after considering one other aspect of the students' approach to 'doing nursing'.

The notions of 'getting through the work' and 'pulling weight' have been discussed already. This approach to doing nursing is relevant here as it has implications for claims to 'profession'. It is convenient here to summarize this approach. There was a tendency for students to regard nursing care as a 'workload' to be got through, and the nursing staff as a 'workforce' to get through it. The students talked of other nurses or students not 'pulling their weight', 'skiving', or not 'mucking in'. This was the picture of nursing which the students painted. It might be captured in the approach to work of one hypothetical student (idealized pastiche of the views of many): 'I'm prepared to get on with a fair share of this nursing work, if you will get on with yours; if we all work together the sooner we will be finished.'

It must be said before going any further that this summarized approach does not seek to deny the existence of finer feelings of altruism among the students. It merely demonstrates the ambiguities which exist in their approach to nursing: it is simply that reasons for being nurses and the hospital system of work are confronted here. The extract below illustrates the point.

KM: One of the things that has come out of these discussions is the idea that nurses are not really wanting to do the work (. . .). It's alright if all the nurses go out and do it, which fits in with the idea that it is alright if the ward sister rolls her sleeves up and the staff nurse will help, in a 'let's go and get on with it' way (. . .). That approach put up against the idea of being a caring professional nurse (. . .) seems like a different thing, one way it sounds like the conveyor belt and the workforce comes in (. . .).

STUDENT: It is a bit like that though.

KM: I'm not saying it in a derogatory sense, maybe it is the only way to see nursing practice. I just wonder if we are not setting up a complication to make it sound like something terribly professional and special.

STUDENT: I think it is a very important point. The other day we were talking amongst ourselves about how people see us and how we felt. It was to do with that programme *Angels* [a BBC drama serial] (. . .), we were thinking they are degrading our profession, we were thinking in a professional way and then started talking about how people see you. People ask you what you do and you say a nurse and they say 'oh, I could never do that'. And you think what exactly do they mean? Do they mean that they wouldn't like to clear up all day, or, 'I really admire your patience and understanding'. And then you realize that they have a false impression – mop brows and clear up. They don't know that there are a lot more technical things that have to be acquired (. . .). There are a lot of complicated things and it does take a lot of teaching as well as the way you treat people, and the general care and attention (. . .).

This student immediately rose to defend the title 'profession' for nursing. My suggestion that to lay claim to profession merely clouded the issue was rejected by the student who went on to adduce evidence, in terms of 'complicated things' in nursing, in support of her claim to profession. Her comment upon the public image of nursing is interesting. She suggests that the public may not see the nurse as a member of a profession, but simply as a 'noble soul' doing a dirty job and therefore standing in need of praise. This attitude verges on patronage.

Differentness

To return to the original question concerning what the students meant by 'profession', the data support the suggestion that student nurses are prepared to describe nursing as a profession, rather than any other type of occupation. What is not quite so clear is upon what grounds they do this. The nature of the work, they would admit, is at times basic and requires little skill, an argument which they support by reference to the fact that unqualified auxiliaries are often doing the same work. Dingwall's discussion of claims to professional status is of some help here.

Dingwall (1976) suggests that the health visitors' claim to 'profession' which he interpreted as a claim to 'a particular kind of social location in relation to other social groups', is not without its problems. In making this claim the health visitor encountered problems which Dingwall describes as 'problems of exclusion and inclusion'. Exclusion, in his context, has to do with defining oneself as a discrete occupation. In the case of Dingwall's health visitors, the work of general nurses and social workers created problems of this kind because their work overlapped with that of the health visitor. Problems of inclusion were posed, on the other hand, by the fact that the occupational groups from which the health visitors wished to distinguish themselves, in terms of work, were the same groups with which they wished to be identified as social equals. Clearly the doctors formed such a group.

The students in the present study are faced with the overlapping of auxiliary work and their own, the auxiliaries being an occupational group from which they wish to distinguish themselves. The data do not provide any clues as to how the students thought that they should rank socially vis-à-vis such occupational groups as the doctors. However, their use of the term 'profession' was indicative of some judgemental process occurring. The students were either using 'profession' in order to claim Becker's notion of some moral respectability for their work, or, as Dingwall suggests in the case of the health visitors, in order to claim social status within the hierarchy of occupations.

The data do not allow any further comment upon which of these alternatives more closely resembles the students' motives. The students certainly seemed to be saying that nursing was in some way different; not 'just another job'. However, in the absence of comparative data, it is impossible to say whether this particular claim is in any way unique to nurses. Again we can make an analytic distinction between the two claims to being 'different'. First, claims can be made on the basis of the work being service oriented, and thereby linked with 'profession' on altruistic grounds. In this sense nurses could claim 'differentness' because they work with sick people, and are thus in a position of privilege and trust. Second, claims to 'differentness' from other occupational groups might well be made on the basis of creativity or craft. The craftsmen who produce works of beauty through skill and long-standing practice, might claim that their work is 'different' from production line work, for example, hand-made reproduction furniture craftsmen as opposed to high street mass produced furniture workers. On this analysis, the student nurses' claims to be doing a 'different' kind of job, not 'just a job', do not necessarily tell us anything about nursing as occupation or profession. In the light of the above discussion, we cannot equate student nurses' claims to 'differentness' with claims to profession.

In this chapter the students' accounts of what constitutes nursing work have been considered. The students are prepared to call certain aspects of their work 'not really nursing'; the aspects of their work which they are prepared to call 'real nursing' tend to be of a technical nature. It has been suggested that this is not unrelated to the possibility that nurses take their kudos from medical work, which is of a more technical nature. 'Real nursing' and 'not really nursing' is a distinction, made by the students, broadly in terms of the age of the patients. Old people who simply need looking after rather than medical attention do not, the data suggest, merit the 'real nursing' label which the acutely ill patients deserve. It could also be argued that the students find it easier to nurse the younger patient, who passes through the ward more quickly, and rewards the student for her efforts by improving and going home relatively quickly. It might be that the student can empathize more readily with a patient who is simply passing through on his way to recovery, than with the long-term chronically sick. This factor might also go some way to explaining why the students tended to have a preference for nursing the acutely ill in surgical wards. In short, it may be easier to empathize with a younger patient who has a transient, curable condition.

Professionalism

Finally, there remains the question of profession. On the one hand, it seems we have a large workforce consisting, for the most part, of the unqualified and the untrained (students and auxiliaries) doing the nursing on the basis of medical prescription. And on the other hand, a small, but ever-growing, academic faction are promoting nursing as a profession independent of medicine. How are the two to be reconciled? The data of this study allow no more than speculation which takes the form of possible extrapolations from the students' understanding of profession. I would suggest that the growing literature concerned with nursing theory is produced by, and serves the needs of, a professionalizing élite in nursing, which is remote from the mainstream.

The behaviour which the students in this study describe as 'professional', is arguably no more than a result of the 'professionalism' which comes from working in the shadow of the medical profession. Freidson's work is helpful here. He maintains that the paraprofessionals' subordination to medicine is made more acceptable to them by their claim to professionalism. This would seem to be one explanation of the position which the student nurses in this study describe. In the light of this discussion, the tension between the professionalizing claims of the nursing theorists and the claims to professionalism by those 'doing nursing' is not as problematic as one might at first suppose. Far from being two opposing perspectives on the same phenomenon, they are, in fact, analytically different claims. The professionalizers, it could be said, are discontented with their lack of autonomy and are striving to achieve professional status in their own right. Thus, nursing diagnosis, prescriptions, and independent practice, in at least some areas of nursing, are the ultimate goals of this group. Those claiming 'professionalism' are content to obscure their lack of professional status proper, by settling for the status conferred upon them by the virtue of working in close association with the medical profession. In Freidson's words:

> 'paramedical occupations hold a distinctly subordinate position in a complex division of labor, dominated by a profession, a position whose character is at once obscured and made palatable by the claim of professionalism.'

> (Freidson 1970a: 70)

The data concerned with 'being professional' presented in this chapter have been discussed in terms of Becker's notion of a 'folk concept' and Freidson's analysis of profession. The folk concept focuses on the meaning intended by those who use the term, in this case student nurses. Freidson's work was drawn upon firstly, because it provides an alternative explanation of the students' use of the term 'profession', and secondly, because he discusses nursing in terms of profession and in relation to the dominant profession of medicine. It remains now to draw the threads of the students' story together and to see what that story tells us about the occupation of nursing and its social organization.

7

CONCLUSIONS AND BEYOND

Introduction

Now that we have seen what the students think nursing is, and also something of the claims which they make for the status of the occupation, we can move on to take a look at the wider occupational group. In doing this we should bear in mind that the students showed some anxiety, if not reluctance, about joining the ranks of nursing. Their anxiety stemmed from the fact that they thought that staff nurse work was intrinsically different from their student work. Also, perhaps more importantly, they realized that they would have to continue to 'fit in', this time in a more enduring sense, into some part of the occupational group – nursing. The students' apprehension is understandable and perhaps best explained by reference to the segmentation of nursing.

As it was suggested in the Introduction, nursing is an occupational group which comprises a wide and diverse range of personnel. The level of education, type of work carried out, and the amount of responsibility shouldered by those calling themselves 'nurse' vary a great deal. This heterogeneity has implications not only for recruitment to the group and the socialization of those recruits, but for the organization and achievements of the group as a whole. In Britain nursing exists, by and large, within the structure of the health service and this means that it has to function alongside other occupational groups which provide other aspects of health care. The most significant of these groups is medicine. A certain amount of interdisciplinary co-operation among these groups is required for them to be an efficient health care service. Some groups, notably medicine, are more powerful than others and there will inevitably be some dispute over territory and mandate. Issues of power and control are an inherent part of the system.

Nursing has to find a suitable public image and internal organization which will allow it to function alongside and in co-operation with these other groups. One problem which nursing has in this respect stems from the fact that there exist, within the occupational group, different aspirations and ambitions for the occupation as a whole. The students' accounts point up the differences in approach to nursing care to be found in the college and on the wards.

These students are by no means the first to note this difference. There has long been an uneasy compromise between *education* and *service*, a compromise which has to be maintained if nurses are to be trained and patients are to be nursed. It is hardly a novel observation that there are differences between the idealized version of the work of an occupation as it is portrayed to its recruits during the process of training and the day-to-day work of its practitioners. As Atkinson (1983) has argued, 'There is no ideal "law", "medicine", "theology" or whatever out there to which the curriculum corresponds as a mere reflection or copy.' Much of what the students preparing to join an occupation learn, then, comes to them in more subtle, complicated, and negotiated ways. An examination of the discontinuities between training and practice makes a starting point from which to ask whether there is one entity – 'nursing' – which students can be taught, one occupational group into which they can be socialized.

Segmentation

Analytically, it is useful to view nursing as a segmented occupational group in which the main segments are *education* and *service* (Bucher and Strauss 1961). The students' accounts suggest that these two segments present them with rather different versions of nursing. An idealized version is promoted by the college, whereas the staff providing the service on the hospital wards practise a rather more pragmatic form of nursing. The college presents what we might call the 'professional' version of nursing, whereas on the wards more of a 'workload' approach was taken. The college, the education segment, is interested in the production of competent registered nurses, capable of independent practice and professional judgement, in so far as this is possible given nursing's relation to medicine. The service, on the other hand, in order to accomplish nursing work, is interested in having students who are competent, but compliant. It might also be said that the goals of the college are long term in the sense of looking to the product of a three-year course. The service's needs, however, are more immediate.

These two versions of nursing are presented to the students in a way which suggests to them that there are competing and conflicting factions within nursing. The students' response, to what is from their perspective a co-existence of two very different versions of nursing, is to negotiate their way through training by learning when and how to reproduce whichever version of nursing is required.

In some sense the students' accounts can be viewed as an elaborate and protracted way of addressing the much vaunted question 'what is nursing?' The answer for the students, in so far as there is one, seems to be that nursing resembles neither the 'professional' nor the 'workload' approach to nursing as canvassed respectively by the education and service segments. This puts into question the whole business of occupational socialization, because students are being socialized into neither version of nursing. Instead they learn to recognize when one form of nursing rather than the other is appropriate, and 'fit in' accordingly. In other words, they learn how to be *student* nurses and not how to be *nurses*.

It is misleading to assume that during training students are learning the ways of the occupation, often they are simply learning how to gain membership: the two are not necessarily entirely compatible. Becker *et al.* (1961) describe 'student culture', and Olesen and Whittaker (1968) discuss the nature of 'studentmanship'. Both these concepts have to do with how students develop perspectives on their day-to-day work which allow them to 'get through' and achieve their long-term goal of gaining the professional qualification. If we are to make some sense of this student view, it has to be located in the wider context of the occupation as a whole. One of the criticisms Atkinson (1983) levels at many studies of occupational socialization is that in their preoccupation with 'situational learning' they attempt to separate the educational experience from the wider issues which concern the profession. One often has, he says, 'little sense, for instance, that the medical school has ultimately to do with any other aspects of the occupation of medicine'. Given the student/worker role which the student of nursing must adopt, it is all the more important that occupational socialization is considered within the wider context of the occupation of nursing.

Carpenter's (1977) work makes a useful starting point from which to view the wider occupational group. In a discussion of the development of the managerial élite within nursing, Carpenter describes three main groups within nursing: 'new managers', 'new professionals', and the 'rank and file'. To these I have added the 'academic professionalizers'. The new managers emerged, according to Carpenter, after the Salmon Report recommendations (DHSS 1966). They operate according to an industrial model of professionalized management and their organizational structure takes the form of bureaucratic line management rather than a collegial model of professional behaviour. The *new professionals* are, as yet, a relatively small group of clinical nurse specialists who emerged, according to Carpenter, as a response to the 'new managerialism'. These clinical specialists, who are independent of line management, stand outside the hierarchical structure of nursing. This clinical development, Carpenter suggests, is modelled on the American notion of the clinical nurse consultant, who 'creams off' the more complex parts of nursing. Carpenter also says that this group of 'new professionals' may well push for the delegation of the more routine work of medicine. The position of clinical specialisms in nursing might be said to have been formalized with the proliferation of post-basic courses and their national recognition in the early 1970s. The *rank and file* can be regarded as the mainstream of nursing. These are nurses who enjoy both doctor-devolved work and the reflected status which comes with working alongside the medical profession. The *academic professionalizers* are to be found in the main in academic circles, and tend to be rather removed from the patients. The work of this group centres mainly on research and the teaching of undergraduate nurses. They seek to achieve autonomy for nursing by elevating the status of 'basic' or 'primary' care, and placing less emphasis upon medically prescribed work. In short, their aim is to promote a style of nursing founded on 'nursing theory', which can take its place among other academic writings, rather than nursing which is founded merely upon tradition and medical dominance.

These four descriptive groups can be considered rather more easily if we adopt as an analytic device the concept of segmentation (Bucher and Strauss 1961, Bucher and Stelling 1977). This allows us to focus upon the interests of each segment, instead of being overly concerned with description. What we have is a straight divide between the *education* segment, which embraces the academic professionalizers and the college tutors, with whom the students come into contact, and the *service* segment, which includes the 'new managers', the 'rank and file', and the 'new professionals'. These two segments canvass distinctly different approaches to the work. Each segment has its more vocal and prominent sections among the membership – the 'academic professionalizers' for the education segment and the 'new managers' for the service. Indeed, it might be more accurate to view the segments in this more narrowly defined way rather than to divide the whole occupational group neatly into just two segments. For the purpose of this analysis, though, I have chosen to view nursing in terms of two segments, each containing more and less committed members. I recognize the limitations of this approach, but proffer it as a start.

The apparent compartmentalization of nursing clearly presents problems for student nurses, who by the very organization of their training have to cross from one segment to another. As the students move between the worlds of education and service, they have to come to terms with two versions of nursing, each with its own rationality and its own structural constraints. These two versions of nursing can exist simultaneously because each segment works within its own structural compartment of the occupation as a whole. By and large, this compartmentalization is successful because the rationale for the practice of one or other version of nursing makes sense within the confines of the structure in which it was conceived. Thus, the service segment's mode of nursing works in so far as it ensures that nursing work gets done; the education segment's 'professional' version of nursing is most credible when it does not have to take account of the realities of the clinical setting.

Both versions of nursing are enforceable on students. The education segment controls the written work, whilst the service segment controls the students' behaviour. Evidence of the students' understanding and ability to reproduce the 'professional' version of nursing, which the educators support, is obtained through the written examination. The service personnel write reports on the students' performance on the wards. The fact that the students cross the boundaries and pass between the service and education segments makes training a point at which the structural compartmentalization of nursing may break down. One of the reasons for looking at the socialization of student nurses in this study was to determine how students manage the structural compartmentalization which confronts them. Segmentation raises wider questions: How do students cope with the segmentation? What are the effects of segmentation on the socialization of students who are at the same time contributing to the nursing workforce? How is conflict over the curriculum to be contained?

There exists a conflict of interests between the college of nursing and the hospital wards which explains the fact that each advocates a different style of nursing. So long as student nurses are to constitute a large part of the workforce, this conflict is inevitable and functional. Control of the curriculum and the process of socialization are clearly important issues. Maintenance of the status quo, whereby students are influenced to a large entent by what they see on hospital wards, has considerable advantages for those responsible for the provision of nursing services. As far as the service segment is concerned, it could be argued that the need for competent student-workers constitutes a sufficiently cogent argument against allowing the education segment, in the form of the colleges of nursing, to take over the control of the curriculum. It is incumbent upon the service segment to persuade the rest of the occupation of this view.

Having mastered the professional nursing rhetoric of the education segment and the practicalities of the service way of nursing, the students discover that, by and large, the best way to get through the training programme is to fit in with the trained staff on the wards. So, while the educators might have the edge on the service segment in so far as they, the educators, are seen to be largely responsible for the control of the training, it seems that, in the students' view, there is more to be gained from accommodating the needs of the service segment. This allegiance is perhaps not surprising since the students, when they qualify, will no longer move between segments, rather they will be located in the service segment.

We have seen from the students' accounts that the notion of 'just passing through' along with 'fitting in' are features of the socialization process. This makes it possible for the students to cross back and forth between the education and service segments, without disturbing the segmentation, or the rationalities upon which it rests. So long as the training programme continues to produce nurses who have a commitment neither to a 'professional' nor a 'workload' version of nursing, but merely a capacity to adapt to a given work organization, nursing is likely to retain these somewhat contradictory segments. Their existence alone is not problematic, for as Bucher and Strauss (1961) point out, the existence of segmentation is inevitable. The competition for curriculum control, however, might very well be a cause for concern.

Ambitions for the occupation

Some of the differences between the segments can be sharpened if we consider what ambitions these segments have for the occupation. Remembering that these ambitions are voiced by the more powerful and active members of the segments, they can best be examined by looking at the usage of the term 'profession'. I shall argue that 'profession' is used in different ways by each segment.

In broad terms we can say that there are different ideas canvassed within nursing, ideas which concern what nursing should look like and what status the occupation should ideally have. First, we have the *service* segment, where the predominant ethos is to get the work done and the way of achieving this is to appeal to the notion of 'profession' with its connotations of duty and compliance. Second, we have an academic group from higher education, within the *education* segment. This group has ambitions for nursing which include making a successful claim to academic and 'professional' status. 'Profession' for this segment holds the same meaning which sociologists would, in general terms, agree upon. Third, we have the students' understanding of nursing. They see it as an occupation which has a certain 'differentness' in the sense that not anyone can do the work. On this count the students are prepared to call nursing a profession, even though they describe much of the work in task-oriented, semi-skilled terms.

There is a problem for nursing if it is to lay a successful claim to 'profession'. The claim is essentially problematic because nursing work is not autonomous, by virtue of the fact that part of nursing's work is dictated by medicine. It also has to be said that nursing is too large and too heterogeneous a group to make any serious claim to professional status.

The service segment, in particular the managers, could be said to be claiming professional status for nursing in order to control the nursing workforce. Whilst a sociologist's notion of profession suggests a more independent worker rather than one who will conform, the nurse managers (and we might include all lines down to the providers of the service on the wards – staff nurses and ward sisters) use the term 'profession' in the sense of professional conduct. In this usage the term has overtones of professional etiquette rather than having to do with occupational status and ideas of independent practice. Once students have been socialized into the ways in which a nurse is expected to behave, managers make appeals to 'professional' behaviour; these become the mainstay of discipline within the nursing service.

It is clear why the managers of the service segment might foster a means of ensuring a compliant workforce. This group, according to Carpenter, sought to professionalize through business administration strategies rather than through their nursing skills. Following their managerial philosophy, the service managers might well form the conclusion that the service does not require independent-practitioner nurses, who are looking for autonomy and freedom of practice. They would favour a workforce that is first and foremost conformist and efficient.

The education segment, led perhaps by the academic minority – some might say élite – can be said to use the same criteria as the sociologists when it comes to defining and claiming professional status. As we have seen, these criteria have to do with autonomy, prestige, and power. Claims to 'profession' in these terms have much more to do with claims to a place in a hierarchy of occupations and in the socio-economic class structure of society than with the nature of the work. The proliferation of literature concerned with nursing theory, a literature which supports the notion of a profession with its body of knowledge, is produced by and serves the needs of a professionalizing élite within academic nursing. This kind of thinking in nursing is clearly different from the 'scientific management' approach to nursing care, which the students encountered in the service segment. Also, any changes in the practice of nursing along the lines suggested by the claims to profession made by the academic group within the education segment, would require a considerable reorganization of the service segment.

Because there is a considerable range of personnel within the service segment, my reservations about making a simple analytic split of nursing into two segments are strongest here. A more sophisticated analysis based on further data would doubtless reveal that several segments are forming within the large service group. Bucher and Strauss (1961) in their discussion of segmentation of the medical profession, suggest that whilst specialties might be thought of as major segments, 'a close look at a specialty betrays its claim to unity, revealing that specialties, too, usually contain segments'.

It is possible to set against these two usages of 'profession' the students' own understanding of 'profession'. As we have seen from their description of the work they carry out in the name of nursing, the students are essentially making a claim to differentness. Nursing for the students is not just any job which anyone can do. They often would not say why nursing deserved a particular distinction in the hierarchy of occupations, or indeed why it is a profession. They did, however, display a tendency to want to set it apart as a rather special occupation. Their claims, as we have seen, come close to Freidson's notion of professionalism, especially as they appear to require some technical overlay or medical sanction for the work which they are prepared to describe as the proper province of nursing.

This view of nursing is probably one which many students carry with them into the ranks of the qualified staff, and so might well be the view held by many within the service segment. Following Bucher and Strauss's idea that there are probably several segments within each major segment, we can argue that there is likely to be a group within the service segment which would hold similar views to those of the students in this study. Indeed the students probably gained their ideas from their contacts with just such staff.

Claims to profession

Three recurrent themes pervade the students' accounts, and illustrate the problematic nature of nursing's claim to 'profession'. First, there is the notion that the student experience fits students for student nurses' work and does not prepare them to be staff nurses. Second, the students described a work organization in which they were frequently interchangeable with nursing auxiliaries; and third, the idea that nursing is influenced, to some extent, by medical dominance.

The student experience of socialization

The students' accounts raise the question of the appropriateness of the three years spent as a student for the eventual work of a staff nurse. In other words how does the student experience help newly qualified staff nurses in their work? We have seen that the students become adept at moving from place to place, they adjust, pick up the routines, and 'get the work done'. The education segment provides a framework for an individualized approach to patient care. However, on the wards the students have found that the care is carried out in the form of routines and that the work is often split up into simple tasks. This militates against individualized nursing care. Exceptions to this are to be found when there is a requirement for complex, more technical care. This tended to be carried out by senior students or staff nurses.

To effect the organization of work according to routines, a qualified member of staff allocates the nursing work on each shift, in a way which has been likened to the 'scientific management' approach which is common in industry. This involves a degradation of labour, and a divorce of the specialist knowledge from the actual carrying out of the tasks. In this way a less skilled workforce can effect the work (Braverman 1974). Student nurses spend three years on the receiving end of this style of organization. On qualifying, they must, in the absence of the charge nurse, be managers of this work organization. The questions raised by the students' accounts of nursing are: How do students make this step from worker to manager? and, How are they prepared for this?

It has already been said that the reaction approach to socialization, which focuses upon the student rather than the occupational role, is appropriate when considering the socialization of the student nurse (Olesen and Whittaker 1968, Becker et al. 1961). The 'fitting in' behaviour described by the students in this study supports the notion that students temporarily abandon their long-term, altruistic, professional-type goals in favour of meeting the requirements of the moment. Becker et al. (1961) say of medical students:

'we believe that the medical students enter medical school openly idealistic about the practice of medicine and the medical profession. They do not lose this idealistic long-range perspective but, realistically develop a "cynical" concern with the day to day details of getting through medical school.'

(Becker *et al.* 1961:422)

Psathas (1968), in a study of student nurses, takes a different view. He preferred not to assign either values or motivational significance to the attitudes of students; rather, he sees expression of a 'realistic' or 'cynical' approach to work as an indication of successful socialization into the occupation. Psathas thought that a realistic or cynical approach to the work demonstrated the adoption of relevant perspectives on the work, and not, as Becker *et al.* would have it, mere situational adaptation. On either analysis, these authors describe the ways in which students behave in the face of the realities which they encounter during the process of 'becoming' doctors and nurses. The tactics they describe represent the students' attempts at 'getting through'.

In this study the notion of 'getting through' has to be seen in the context of working on the wards, receiving satisfactory ward reports, and passing examinations. Interestingly, the students made little reference to the written examinations which they had to pass in order to achieve registration. They appeared to consider themselves to be part of the workforce on the wards and were therefore much more oriented to 'fitting in' and 'getting through' there. The student experience in the education segment appears to be inappropriate for the preparation of staff nurses on two counts. First, it does not offer a style of nursing which accords with the reality of life on the wards and, second, it does not prepare the students for this discontinuity. We can only speculate about why the students placed little emphasis on written examinations. When they were mentioned, it was in a general 'exams make me nervous' sense; rather than in any attempt to discuss their relevance to registration. In contrast, the medical students in Becker's work tried to approach the examinations in an 'intelligent' way, by electing to learn topics which would be of use in subsequent practice as well as get them through their examinations. Since there were too many topics and subjects to cover, the Kansas medical students were faced with making choices about what to learn and what to cut out. Eventually, Becker *et al.* argue, the students concerned themselves with discovering what the teaching staff expected of them, and then concentrated upon learning that.

There are interesting differences between the approach to the 'theoretical' part of the student experience taken by the students that I interviewed, and that found in Becker's work. The medical students take it for granted that all of the theory they are taught is of some use, but suppose that some parts will be of more use than others in their future practice. However, as Becker points out, the medical students have little experience of practice so are unable to select which parts to learn for examinations, using future utility as a criterion of selection. They were, however, able to discover what the faculty expected them to know and concentrated upon learning that; this tactic resolved their difficulty in selecting topics to learn for examinations (Becker *et al.* 1961). The students I interviewed were familiar with nursing on the wards and, therefore, were also aware of the fact that the 'theory' is of little practical help to them. The student nurses know what the education segment expects of them in terms of examination performance; what they are much less sure of is what the ward sisters expect of them in terms of practical performance. It is therefore entirely reasonable that they should place such emphasis on 'fitting in' and 'getting through' on the wards, as this is most appropriate to their situation.

There is an interesting question of power behind this issue. The student nurses were not always sure just what was expected of them by the individual ward sisters; this they had to find out when they reached the ward. Also, the students clearly had the impression that the sisters either liked or did not like certain students and that this had as much to do with personality as with anything else. Thus, the students were really charged with the task of meeting the expectations of those above them both on the wards and in the college. However one construes the students' position, whether as students, workers, or apprentices, their progress is contingent upon their creating a favourable impression upon those further up the hierarchy.

Student to staff nurse

As we have seen, Becker *et al.* (1961) suggest that students come into a profession with an idealized view of the attitudes, values, and knowledge of its members. By means of interaction with the members of the profession and an exposure to its teachings, the students can adjust their ideals by reference to the reality. The major difficulty facing student nurses appears to be the practical one of how they will function when they become staff nurses. Thus, the main thrust of this discussion is not so much concerned with how the student nurses adopt professional attitudes, values, and the like, but rather with how they learn to function as staff nurses. This is an important question to address as the eventual achievement of registration and qualification is the aim of the three years spent as a student. The 'professional' role, towards which their socialization is aimed, seems to the students to be different from the student role which they have taken for three years, different, not merely in terms of status but in terms of content. According to the students, the staff nurses' work is further removed from the patients, especially when the staff nurse has to take charge of the ward in the absence of the ward sister.

It has already been noted that anticipatory socialization is not a particularly helpful notion in considering the student nurse's training for work as a staff nurse. The students, when faced with questions about how they might deal with a situation when they were staff nurses, tended to take a 'cross that bridge when we come to it' approach. It is the dictates of the immediate situation and meeting the day-to-day requirements that are the real priorities of the student world. So the main transition that the student nurse must make on becoming a staff nurse, is from a worker undertaking allocated tasks to a qualified member of staff, allocating work.

It has been suggested that the ward sister adopts a 'bureaucratic' rather than a 'professional' solution to the problem of supervision of untrained and unqualified staff. Students have had the opportunity to see this style of management in action, but have not practised it themselves. There is a tension between two versions of nursing: the college-taught 'professional' version with individualized care using professional judgement and the 'workload' version, with its bureaucratic means of getting work done. In practice at least, the tension is resolved, in a fairly arbitrary way. That is to say, the students learn from the education segment the rhetoric of individualized care and the bases for professional judgement, yet they soon discover that this does not work on the wards, where the sister commonly adopts a 'bureaucratic' approach in order to achieve her ends in patient care. The students found that the individualized care approach was inappropriate on the wards and so had to adapt to the ways in which the qualified staff organized the nursing, invariably by routines. The students soon reached a point where they were prepared to justify the discrepancy between what they were taught and what they saw; the justification was made on the basis of expediency in the face of shortages of staff and time.

There are difficulties for occupational socialization inherent in the 'bureaucratic' solution to the supervision of work. These lie in the deskilling of the work. The difficulties have particularly to do with how the students learn to apply their knowledge in order to make professional judgements. It has been argued that trained staff solve the problem of having to achieve nursing work through unqualified and untrained workers, by resorting to splitting up the nursing work into tasks and nursing by routines. Also, we have seen that the students have some notion of how to function as staff nurses because they have observed staff nurses at work. The students do not, however, get a chance to see how the education segment's notion of professional judgement is translated into the service segment's bureaucratic organization of care on the wards. In other words, where the ward sister determined the patients' care, on the basis of her professional judgement, and then translated the overall plan into a set of routines to be undertaken by the students and auxiliaries, the students can only observe the resultant bureaucratic model. The professional judgement was an invisible process which the sister used to produce the plans for the care of the patients.

The newly qualified staff nurse is most likely to organize the work on the basis of 'routines' learned as a student. On the face of it two approaches which staff nurses might take to 'getting work done' might appear to be the same. In the first, if they simply supervise the carrying out of routines, which they have seen tried and tested, then conceptually staff nurse work is not so very different from that undertaken as a student. However, with the second approach, the staff nurse works from first principles, and applies theoretical knowledge which she acquired as a student, and in this way she arrives at decisions about patient care. In other wards, professional judgement is in play. These decisions may then be carried out in a bureaucratic way, using routines. The data tend to suggest that the students regard the 'theoretical' input from the education segment as an irrelevance on the wards; this would render the 'first principles' approach to nursing an unlikely option for the staff nurse. In practice, it is not so easy to separate the two notions of a 'workload' – the bureaucratically organized approach, and the 'professional' approach to nursing. Indeed, the two concepts are interrelated because of the organizational context in which nursing is carried out.

When a 'bureaucratic' solution is adopted there is an assumption that the 'manager' is employing professional judgement. This assumption, as we have already hinted, is open to question. A newly qualified staff nurse has not had the experience or the opportunity to practise and can not therefore transfer, overnight, from routine to professional judgement. There is then, the possibility that this transition never takes place, in which case nursing would be practised on the basis of tried and tested routines, handed down from the days of their formulation, when the ward sisters were women of long-standing experience. If this is the case, the three years spent in training can almost be seen in terms of the students working their way up the ranks, in order that they might assume command when they have put in the requisite number of years, and achieved registration. This, it could be argued, is an expensive use of personnel. An analogy with the armed forces is not out of place in a discusssion of the nursing service. The army recruits its leaders, by and large, from a different section of the population from the one providing recruits to the ranks. Nursing, it seems, uses its future 'officers', along with auxiliary staff, to carry out a large volume of nursing work.

The questions raised here concerning the socialization of the staff nurse and the preparation for the role of a qualified nurse, have to do with the structure and content of the training. The emphasis which the students themselves placed upon 'fitting in' and 'getting through' demonstrates the fact that the three years are seen in terms of short spells in different clinical areas with a constant awareness of the next move. For anticipatory socialization to occur the students would need to spend longer periods of time in one place and to take more responsibility than is at present the case; in this way their work would more closely resemble that of the staff nurse. The present situation is almost the opposite state of affairs in that the students become used to being highly mobile and taking little responsibility; they are then faced with having to settle down in one ward and play a part in running it.

In short, it seems that the student experience does not prepare the student for the work of a staff nurse. Instead it prepares them for picking up different ways of working and for 'fitting in' with any given system of nursing and importantly, to 'get the work done'. The original question – Does three years of 'fitting in' prepare the student to be a qualified nurse? – remains. There seems to be at least some room for manoeuvre in the staff nurses' work. The extent of this discretion is dependent, in part, upon what they make of it, and in part upon how far the charge nurse expects the staff nurse to 'fit in'. It must also be remembered that this discussion of the staff nurse role is based on accounts of student nurses. Their future performance as registered nurses, and indeed their view after registration, could well differ from their present accounts. The students' accounts do, however, represent a defensible picture of ward organization. So long as nursing care is carried out in an institution where thirty or more patients are the responsibility of a small number of qualified staff, assisted by auxiliaries and students, a 'workload' approach to care is defensible, and possibly inevitable.

Interchangeability of students and auxiliaries

The students frequently mentioned that they are interchangeable with the auxiliaries as members of the nursing workforce. The important part which the auxiliaries play in the students' lives has been a recurrent theme in the students' story. The notion of interchangeability of students and auxiliaries is problematic when it comes to nursing's claim to 'profession'. There is a school of thought which argues that nursing auxiliaries should not be referred to as 'nurses', because they are not qualified members of that occupational group. However, these data, supported by others (Baker 1978, Hardie 1980), suggest that nursing auxiliaries are indeed doing the work. It is, therefore, unhelpful to argue along nominalist lines of 'these are nurses, they do the nursing, these are not nurses, ergo their work is not nursing work'.

Nursing work could be better described as work done for and to patients. If this approach is taken, then it is possible to look at the different aspects of 'patient work' and decide who might best carry it out, rather than call it nursing work and look to a nurse to do it. Hughes (1971:312–13) says, in a discussion of 'nurses' work':

> 'Some may think that nurses are a bit presumptious in daring to describe everybody else's work in order to learn what is their own. But that is the only way to do it well . . . an occupation or a job consists of a bundle of tasks. The thing that holds them together is that they are all done by one person and under a single name. A person, a name and a bundle of tasks. . . . Why are the tasks in this bundle done by the person who is called a nurse? For not all the tasks in the bundle require the same degree of skill.'

At the extremes of 'patient work' are the complex technical aspects of care introduced by the advances of medical technology and the less tangible psycho-social aspects of care. The former, it is not denied, must be carried out by trained personnel, whether 'nurse' training is appropriate or desirable for these aspects of care is another matter. Technological advances in medicine bring with them new breeds of technicians. This has already been seen in operating theatres with the introduction of anaesthetic technicians.

The psycho-social aspects of patient care, it is increasingly claimed, must be undertaken by educated nurses. However, it is the case that there is a wide range of work undertaken in the name of 'nursing', much of which is undertaken by nursing auxiliaries (Johnson 1978). Not only did the students realize that they were in many instances interchangeable with auxiliaries, but the students sometimes felt that the trained staff held the auxiliaries in higher esteem. The auxiliaries are a stable element of the ward workforce, they know the ward well, have no formal training needs, and are, therefore, often more efficient and less demanding of the trained staff than are the students. Also, the auxiliary is one of the key figures in the student's occupational socialization. The students freely admit that on entering a ward they would seek advice from the auxiliary in their attempt to 'fit in' and 'get through'. Hardie's work (1978) supports this view of the auxiliary as an important member of the nursing workforce.

The interchangeability of student nurses and auxiliaries has implications for both the cost of the nursing service and the future development of the occupation. Whilst the latter is the main concern here, it is interesting to note in passing the economic questions raised, as these will, one way or another, have some influence on the occupation's development. Mercer (1979: 89) has shown that newly qualified nurses are a highly mobile group. They are, however, mobile within the service. About one quarter of nurses contribute to the annual 'turnover', that is move into, between, or out of positions in the health service each year. Mercer found little movement into other occupations or beyond the NHS, although this last point is likely to change with increasing opportunities beyond the state provision. Essentially the nurse 'turnover' pattern is one of 'in and out of work'. Currently those in training contribute 20 per cent to hospital nursing and midwifery staff (UKCC 1985). Taking failure and drop-out rate into account, 65 per cent of those who start training ultimately reach the register (Hutt et al. 1985). Reid (1985) has linked qualified staff wastage with a reliance on student labour. The wards are so dependent upon mobile labour – students and 'bank' or agency nurses – that the resultant discontinuity drives qualified staff away. Demographic trends are also clearly important when we look at recruitment to nursing.

Hardie (1978) suggested that the major trade off in nursing employment is between qualified staff and auxiliaries. Where there are many registered nurses there are few auxiliaries and vice versa. It is not entirely clear what the implications of this employment pattern are, but, coupled with the interchangeability of the students and auxiliaries it could be seen as a warning light to professionalizers and a possible attraction to planners and policy makers. Hardie (1980: 229) found that the extent to which health districts could rely upon student labour appeared to be the strongest determinant of the number of auxiliaries that would also be required. More recent figures (UKCC 1986) suggest that whilst there was a steep rise in the contribution from auxiliary staff prior to 1974, there has been an erratic pattern since then with a recent decline. The picture is perhaps best summed up in the work of Bosanquet and Gerard (1985), which states that the grading mix, including dependence upon students, is highly variable and needs to be taken account of in future planning.

According to the students I interviewed, it would appear that a good deal of nursing work is carried out by unqualified staff. Students not only do much of the same work as auxiliaries, but they are often taught by the auxiliaries. It would perhaps make sense to argue that nursing should move towards employing more auxiliary nurses, supervised along 'scientific management' principles, with the planning being separated from the delivery of care, in all but the complex technical areas of the work. The 'scientific managers' would require rather more in terms of preparation than simply spending three years as a worker and then 'getting to be in charge'. At present, the division of labour between trained and untrained staff is obscured by the presence of student nurses.

If Hardie (1980) is right and it is the case that when nursing auxiliaries are not being employed and students are not available, then the only option is to employ qualified staff, then the question to be asked is how far can nursing insist that 'nursing' work *must* be done by qualified nurses? The answer to this question is often couched in terms of patient safety, yet it hides a good deal of occupational imperialism. Student nurses, by virtue of their 'preprofessional' status and ongoing education, whilst they are not qualified, manage to give the workforce a 'professional gloss' which the auxiliaries cannot offer. In this respect students and auxiliaries are not interchangeable.

Johnson (1978) suggests that the 'dirty work',[1] in nursing is carried out by the students and the auxiliaries. The two groups handle this situation differently. The students can either leave, or regard their place in the hierarchy as a temporary one from which they hope one day to emerge and go on to supervise other workers who will do the 'dirty work'. The auxiliaries do not have this option, they must either leave or stay. Sheer lack of alternative employment does not give the auxiliary any more choice. It is 'dirty work' or unemployment. The students are confronted daily, in their contacts with the auxiliaries, with a contradiction. They experience doing the same work as the auxiliaries, yet they have received, from the education segment, ideas which encourage them to view their work in a different way – in a 'professional' way.

Medical dominance

We mentioned at the outset that nursing is carried out alongside other health care disciplines and the fact that medicine has gained a

---

[1] 'Dirty work' is essentially being used in the sense that Everett Hughes used it to mean the routine unskilled work. In nursing it may well also be dirty in the everyday sense of the word.

position of professional dominance in this multidisciplinary approach to health care. The students in this study expressed a preference for work in the more technical, fast-moving, and medically dominated areas of nursing. In short, they prefered technical, doctor-devolved work. It must be borne in mind that this preference might simply reflect the stage of their development, both as adults and nurses. Nevertheless, in the absence of contradictory evidence, it is reasonable to accept the students' stated preference for the type of nursing which has medical connections, and is thus regarded as 'prestigious' work (Hughes 1971, Freidson 1970). Just as nurses have sloughed off their 'dirty work' to the auxiliaries, they have welcomed medical work. This is largely because it represented special skills and responsibilities which allowed them to enjoy the reflected glory of the dominant profession of medicine. This 'prestigious' work assisted them, some would contend, in their efforts to become professionals. With Freidson I would argue that the nurses' only hope with such a venture is to achieve what he has called professionalism, that is a kind of look-alike professional status without the power, or indeed the status of the traditional professions. This taking work from above, in the hope of rising, and sloughing work off below is by no means a new phenomenon. Hughes (1971) in a discussion of 'social role and the division of labour' said:

'the ranking has something to do with the relative clean-ness of the functions performed. The nurses, as they successfully rise to professional standing, are delegating the more lowly of their traditional tasks to aides and maids. . . . As medical technology develops and changes, particular tasks are constantly downgraded; that is, they are delegated by the physician to the nurse. The nurse in turn passes them on to the maid. But the occupations are being up-graded, within certain limits. The nurse moves up nearer to the doctor in techniques and devotes more of her time to supervision of other workers.'

(Hughes 1971: 307)

The students in this study expressed interest in the technical aspects of their work, placing a greater importance on the medical knowledge, rather than on the 'nursing' they were taught. In short, they succumbed to medical dominance. This attitude is consistent with the status claims described by Hughes. Nurses, then, can seek to enhance their status by taking on managerial tasks (Carpenter

1977) or technical tasks (Hughes 1971). Hughes also acknowledged that nurses would have more time to devote to the managerial work of supervision. However, the main thrust of his argument has to do with the adoption of technical tasks by nurses. It is helpful in this discussion to conceive of 'technical' and 'managerial' tasks separately. The important point to note is that neither of these activities constitutes nursing work. The attraction which either avenue holds for those seeking professional status for nursing, is that the work does not fall into the realms of 'anyone can do it' work: work which could be carried out by nursing auxiliaries.

The students appeared to be content with the reflected 'professionalism' which is gained from the close working relationship with the medical profession. The area in which nursing is most likely to gain a foothold for independent practice is the care of the elderly or long term sick. These specialties have several attractions for the professionalizing nurse. They are not overly popular with doctors and there is not a great deal of diagnosis and treatment involved in the conventional medical sense. Care, rather than cure, social as well as clinical well-being are the goals. This is not to suggest that the social well-being of patients does not concern the medical staff in other specialties. Indeed the care/cure distinction is something of a 'straw man' and is only of any use as an expression of emphasis rather than as an empirical reality. It is simply the case that when cure becomes an impossible goal because of multiple pathology and degenerative diseases of old age, the potential for improvement tends to lie in daily living and social activities. Much of this kind of work can be achieved by nurses making assessments, setting goals, and working towards them in order to help the patients reach their full potential. This is part and parcel of the rhetoric of the education segment's professional version of nursing. Yet it has to be said that for the students in this study, whilst they expressed a surprise liking for geriatrics, by far the most popular area was the surgical ward, where there is usually more technical work.

It is not the intention here to argue the case for the professionalizers, or for those content to bask in 'professionalism'. The point is simply that the student nurses in this study, following Carpenter's 'rank and file', showed little interest in divorcing their work from medicine. They were, in fact, happy to describe certain aspects of patient care as doctors' business, for instance, telling the patients their diagnoses and prognoses, or giving information about their condition. This willingness to subordinate nursing to medicine was not seen by the students to detract from nursing in any way. The students were, by and large, content to accept that it was the doctors' place to decide what 'their patients' should be told about their condition and the students would fall in line with that. Such subordination, it could be argued, is evidence of the students surrendering any claim to professional autonomy. Such an argument turns on the analyst's perspective on profession, whether it be a 'trait' or a functionalist's approach or Becker's notion of a 'folk concept'. It could also be said, setting aside the finer details of the analytic debate, that the students' view was a realistic one. They recognize medical dominance for what it is and do not allow it to interfere with their conception of nursing. This realistic view is summed up by Freidson (1970a: 76) who argued that the dominant position of medicine frustrates any efforts which the 'para-professionals' make towards securing full professional autonomy.

> 'It might be noted that paraprofessional occupations usually seek professional status by creating many of the same institutions as those which possess professional status. They develop a formal standard curriculum of training, hopefully at a university. They write codes of ethics. They are prone to seek support for licensing or registration so as to be able to exercise some control over who is allowed to do their work. But what they persistently fail to attain is full autonomy in formulating their training and licensing standards and in actually performing their work. Their autonomy is only partial, being second-hand and limited by a dominant profession.'

The trappings of profession are present, but the autonomy, it seems, is unattainable so long as the profession of medicine dominates. One of the striking features of the students' accounts was their lack of concern to rid themselves of medical dominance; in fact, they seemed rather to cling to it and take the medical position as their point of reference, or indeed their sanction.

Nursing as profession or craft

I have set out these three main themes from the students' story in this rather protracted way because they are important if we are to consider the future of nursing as an occupation. Nursing, it seems, has problems on almost any analysis, when it seeks to lay claim to the status of profession. Whichever meaning 'profession' carries – the students' 'differentness' (Freidson's professionalism), a symbol to which appeal can be made for compliant behaviour, or professional status within a hierarchy of occupations – the claim is somewhat weakened by the presence of large numbers of auxiliaries who are unqualified, yet doing nursing work.

An occupational group as heterogeneous as nursing is bound to run into difficulties in the socialization of its recruits. The most obvious question is, how do students cope when they discover that there exists more than one version of the group's work? We have seen how the student nurses reacted to this – they 'fit in' with whatever is required at the time and produce the appropriate version of nursing. But there is also the question of the vested interests of the different segments. It is reasonable to suppose that if the segments have particular ambitions for the occupation, it will be to the advantage of each segment to promote its own version of the work. The different segments will, therefore, have different expectations of the socialization process. Indeed, it is worth asking if the segments can be accommodated in a heterogeneous occupational group, without harming that group. In looking at the segments within an occupational group the interest lies not in determining which approach or ideology is right or wrong, but in asking why it is that some ideologies gain support and are promoted, whilst others are not. If there is a struggle between segments for hegemony, it may not be in the best interests of the occupation as a whole, or of those it serves.

A segmented occupational group has to find ways of containing its differences when it operates publicly. In other words whilst differences of ideology and work organization may be possible to sustain within the group, when it comes to its dealings with other health care disciplines the group must be able to produce and rely upon a united front. Whilst it seems rather far removed from nursing's organizational structure, Evans-Pritchard's (1940) study of the African Nuer's political system sheds some light on segmentation. The largest political segment is the tribe, which is divided into a number of territorial segments. These segments are more than geographical divisions, as the members of each see themselves as distinct communities and act accordingly. Evans-Pritchard's (1940: 142) description cannot be bettered:

'Segments of a tribe have many of the characteristics of the tribe itself. . . . Each segment is itself segmented and there is opposition between parts. The members of any segment unite for war against adjacent segments of the same order and unite with these adjacent segments against larger sections:

He goes on:

'The tendency towards fusion is inherent in the segmentary character of the Nuer political structure, for although any group tends to split into opposed parts these parts must tend to fuse in relation to other groups since they form part of a segmentary system.'

(Evans-Pritchard 1940: 148)

Clearly we are not talking of war between the segments within the occupation of nursing. However, the notion of various internal differences existing within an occupation is useful. The united front is clearly required when nursing deals with other groups. The students learn not to expose the differences as they pass between segments during their training – instead, they 'fit in' and move on.

It is difficult, and ultimately unhelpful, to draw any succinct conclusions from this analysis of the students' wide-ranging accounts of nursing. I am conscious of the fact that one response to this detailed exposition of the student nurses' world might well be to say 'now what?', or even 'so what?' I will conclude, then, by posing the question which, as I see it, nursing urgently needs to address. Stated briefly, this would be: How best can such a heterogenous group as nurses be organized in order to provide its service? From this stems a further question – Should nurses continue as this heterogeneous group, making various claims to profession?

It seems that there are at least two possible alternative structures which nurses might consider. The first scenario involves a reduction in number, and a rise in educational standards. The aim would be to produce 'professional' nurses charged with effecting patient care through a mixed workforce, which would include some grade of trained nursing auxiliary. The effort would, then, be directed towards the production of 'scientific manager' sisters, rather than, as is currently the case, producing large numbers of nurses, many of whom function at a lower level than the one proposed here. With a smaller and more homogeneous group, educated to a higher level, claims to 'profession' might be more successful. At the moment the sheer numbers involved make claims to professional status little more than pipe dreams. The second option would involve a drawing away from attempts to gain professional status for nursing. Instead nursing would be characterized as a craft. Emphasis would be placed on the perfection of the skilled work of nursing and less stress placed on achieving a place for the occupation among 'the professions'.

Much of the work on 'primary' nursing concentrates on the promotion of an activity independent of medicine. The delineation and maintenance of this independent part of nursing is problematic. The rhetoric is stronger than the reality. MacFarlane (1976) described primary nursing in similar terms to those found in Virginia Henderson's (1966) definition of nursing, emphasizing as it does that nursing is essentially the business of assisting others to do what they would otherwise do for themselves. This, MacFarlane stressed, involves both simple and complex acts. Concentrating more upon getting these acts right, and less on the theoretical writings, might serve to advance nursing care rather more than the writings of the nurse theorists have so far managed to do.

Nurse theorists derive their satisfaction from the intellectual exercise of promoting nursing as an autonomous activity, which is free of medical dominance. Whether or not this group would sustain their interest if they were to find themselves practising according to their reconstruction of 'basic nursing care' is probably another matter. But the question still remains. Is this intellectual activity undertaken for altruistic reasons concerning patient welfare, or is it a means of achieving academic and professional status for nursing (which would perhaps be no bad thing). Professional status brings with it power, and this could be an important factor in getting the provision of nursing care right for the changing needs of the population.

A concentration on skills, with appropriate reference to theoretical ideas, would fit nicely into the craftsman approach to nursing. Craftsmen, having served an apprenticeship, are the masters of their trade or craft. Braverman (1974:443) in his discussion of degraded work, catalogues the demise of the craftsman who he says was 'tied to the technical and scientific knowledge of his time in the daily practice of his craft'.

Characterization of nursing as a craft would entail less emphasis upon drawing away from medicine. There would, nevertheless, be organizational implications. Braverman's (1974:443) comment is pertinent here:

> 'For the worker the concept of skill is traditionally bound up with craft mastery – that is to say, the combination of knowledge of materials and processes with the practised manual dexterities required to carry out a specific branch of production. The breakup of craft skills and the reconstruction of production as a collective or social process have destroyed the traditional concept of skill and opened up only one way for mastery over labor processes: in and through scientific, technical and engineering knowledge. . . . What is left to workers is a reinterpreted and woefully inadequate concept of skill: a specific dexterity, a limited and repetitious operation "speed as skill", etc.'

A concentration on craft and skills would produce a nursing workforce which could operate along the lines Stinchcombe (1959) describes in the construction industry. These were skilled craftsmen who needed little in the way of supervision in their tasks as their work is guided by standards of craftsmanship, which Stinchcombe argues are similar to professional standards.

As things stand, though, the occupational group which operates under the name 'nursing' must accept, if it is to continue as one group, that there exists within it a wide range of interests, skills, and academic ability. Much of the difficulty in defining what nursing is, both in terms of activity and professional status, lies in the heterogeneity of the group. Recognition of the abilities and limitations, and of the ambitions and motivations of the different segments within the totality of nursing provides at least a starting point from which to consider the furture of nursing as a united group. Nursing's future will, to a large extent, also be dependent upon the changes both within the medical profession and society as a whole. Changes in age structure, disease patterns, population trends, economic and social constraints which result in less emphasis on the technological and more on the social and community-based aspects of care will, in all probability, lead to nursing coming into the forefront of health care. In this event there must exist a united nursing service, which will not only be able to represent its needs at government level, but will also be able to provide care of all kinds, requiring different levels of skill, safely and efficiently.

Nursing is at present in a state of change. The United Kingdom Central Council for Nursing Midwifery and Health Visiting has published its Project 2000 Report, which sets out the way forward for the development of nursing education and the structure of the service. The Project 2000 Report recognizes that the link between education and service in nursing is an unsatisfactory arrangement for both education and service provision and recommends a new approach to education and nursing organization. The latter, it proposes, should be based upon a practitioner-centred division of labour. The Report touches upon the kinds of issues raised in this analysis of the students' world, issues which will doubtless be debated for some time to come. As this analysis was completed before Project 2000, I have not attempted to integrate the two, rather I have restricted myself to drawing attention to the commonality of issues, and simply offer it as a further dimension to the debate.

Any consideration of nursing has to be set into the organizational context of the NHS, which is in the throes of yet another reorganization as it introduces general managers and an industrial style of management in order to achieve a more cost-effective health service (Griffiths 1983). Clearly there is some way to go, both with Project 2000 and Griffiths-style management implementation. Nursing will have to consider its own internal reorganization carefully if it is not to find that, once again, its future has been determined from outside. General managers will have a strong voice in determining the mix of personnel to be employed in the nursing sectors of their operations.

It is important to note that the ambitions and end goals that an occupational group has in its sights, are very likely to have an effect upon the development and the eventual character of that group. We should then ask, What will nursing eventually look like if it follows its current quest, albeit in various guises, for professional status? We should also ask, What would the occupational group look like if it had ambitions other than to gain professional status? The pursuit of a body of knowledge and the development of theoretical writings in the hope that these will secure nursing a favourable place within the hierarchy of occupations, will bring with it certain consequences. It may, for instance, lead to a stratified system of nursing care which, in turn, leads to the emergence of some new care group with its own organization and ambitions for training and certification. In the increasingly capitalist/rationalist approach to the provision of health care, this would be an important development as far as nursing is concerned. It does not take too much imagination to speculate about the financial attractions in employing a less qualified, cheaper labour force to undertake nursing work. A less status-conscious group with different ambitions might provide a service better suited to society's needs.

It is not the intention here to speculate in detail but, more appropriately, to suggest that the nature of the ambitions fostered and advanced by an occupational group have far-reaching consequences for its future. Ultimately, it is an occupation's ambitions and self-image that will, more than anything else, shape the nature of the work it undertakes or the service it provides. In the case of nursing, the occupation's views on the status of the auxiliary workers who undertake patient care will be crucial in the restructuring of the group. Debates about nursing's self-image, about professionalism and professional status, extend well beyond semantics. The organizational structure and, indeed, the survival of nursing as an occupational group depend upon the outcome of such deliberations.

APPENDIX:
RESEARCH STRATEGY

The approach adopted for this study comes within the scope of ethnography. Based firmly within the Weberian tradition of 'verstehen', this method draws upon the interactionist perspective (Weber, trans. Henderson and Parsons 1947, Blumer 1969, Rock 1979). Specifically, the data comprise forty tape-recorded informal interviews which I carried out with student nurses at various stages of their three-year training. The students expressed opinions upon a wide range of topics, so it will help to put their accounts of their work and training into some context if I describe the manner and the spirit in which the data were obtained and handled. First, though, a general note about the qualitative approach, followed by a discussion of its use in this study.

The main concern was to get student nurses to express, in a spontaneous way, their ideas about nursing. This interest led me to employ a qualitative interpretive research method. The merits of this style of research have been well documented (see Denzin 1970, Filstead 1970). Perhaps the most elaborate account of this method is that supplied by Glaser and Strauss in their oft quoted *The Discovery of Grounded Theory* (1967), upon which this study was in large part modelled. The central idea in the generation of grounded theory is that theory is generated from and grounded in data by a process of induction. The data are coded according to conceptual categories which are suggested by the data themselves. In this way the categories are developed and refined so that they can eventually be written up as theory. Lest this should sound too grandiose, it is worth stating here what Glaser and Strauss understand by 'theory'. They define it as 'a strategy for handling data in research, providing modes of conceptualization for describing and explaining' (Glaser and Strauss 1967: 3).

This inductive means of generating a theory is by no means new. Znaniecki described the process of analytic induction in 1934, and elaborations of the method can be found in the work of Robinson (1951) and Cressey (1950). Znaniecki's (1934) analytic induction is concerned with the generation and proof of theories which account for specific phenomena. Glaser and Strauss offer a systematic means of handling qualitative data, namely, the 'constant comparative method'. The 'constant comparative method' does not insist upon universality or proof. Glaser and Strauss (1967:39) argue that: 'Generating hypotheses requires evidence enough to establish a suggestion – not an excessive piling up of evidence to establish a proof and the consequent hindering of the question of the generation of a new hypothesis.' The intention is to generate and *suggest*, but not *test* hypotheses. The 'constant comparative method', as the name suggests, works by comparing each item of data with the categories which are, or have been developed, and seeing whether they fit. The data collection and analysis are carried out side by side and in this way the direction of the study is dictated by the emergent categories and theory. Glaser and Strauss recommend a technique which they call 'theoretical sampling', which they describe as 'the process of data collection for generating theory whereby the analyst jointly collects, codes and analysis his data and decides what data to collect and where to find them, in order to develop his theory as it emerges'.

The method employed in this study comes closest to the 'constant comparative method', as there was no 'hypothetical formulation of the phenomenon' which analytic induction demands. There was instead a generalized interest in the student nurses' world, along with some thoughts about the organization of work on hospital wards and communication between nurses and hospital patients. These thoughts on the study had been developed in the course of a previous research project (Moult, Hockey and Melia 1978).

There is a fair amount of scope for interpretation within the *Discovery of Grounded Theory*. For example, at the end of the discussion of 'theoretical sampling', Glaser and Strauss say that:

> 'since each researcher is likely to encounter special conditions in his research, he will inevitably add to the discussion of theoretical sampling . . . we would scarcely wish to limit this type of comparative analysis to what we can say about it, from either our own research or our knowledge of others' research. We have merely opened the topic.'

I have taken up this invitation and assumed that 'theoretical sampling' could be used in my study, even though I did not collect data from any group other than the student nurses I interviewed. I used the idea that emergent categories dictate the direction and nature of further data collection by allowing the categories which emerged from the early interviews to determine the topics covered in later ones. Bucher and Stelling (1977), in their longitudinal study of students undertaking postgraduate training, held that they could not use 'theoretical sampling' because they were committed to using the same cohort of students. They maintained that 'theoretical sampling would have entailed moving on to new research sites which provide the kinds of data needed to test emerging ideas and problems'. The question of whether 'theoretical sampling' is an appropriate term for the research tactics I employed turns, I think, on the question of what directed the development of the study, rather than precisely where the data came from. The ideas the interviews produced in the early stage of the study served to shape the line of enquiry, and in this way the data collection was directed by the theoretical notions which emerged.

Informal interviews

Participant observation is perhaps the most conventional field-work method employed in qualitative research. Long periods of observation in the natural setting allow the researcher to gain insights into the world of those being studied. The informal interview also allows the interviewer to understand the inform-ants' world from their perspective. Participant observation and the interview will never do exactly the same job. Becker and Geer (1957) state most emphatically that:

> 'the most complete form of sociological datum, after all, is the form in which the participant observer gathers it. . . . Partici-pant observation can thus provide us with a yardstick against which to measure the completeness of data gathered in other ways.'

This overstates the case. As Trow (1957) argues, 'different kinds of information about man and society are gathered most fully and economically in different ways and . . . the problem under investigation properly dictates the method of investigation'.

The close involvement of the researcher in the production of data is as true of the informal interview as it is of participant observation, indeed participant observation involves *de facto* a considerable amount of informal or 'natural' interviewing. The field data produced are handled in much the same way that the fieldnotes of participant observation might be. The distinction often made in the literature, notably by Becker and Geer, between the interview and participant observation, is perhaps more of an empirical than a conceptual distinction when it comes to considering data collection and analysis.

In the informal interviews in this study the students described their experiences of becoming nurses, and, in a sense, could be said to be replaying events from their nursing world for the benefit of the researcher. It should also be noted that as a nurse as well as a sociologist I was, to some degree, familiar with the world that the students described. This inside knowledge can clearly bring problems and it could not be said that I entered the research situation as a 'naïve observer'. Indeed, that particular ploy would not have been available to me, if I were to maintain my credibility.

The informal interview sits more comfortably among other ethnographic strategies than alongside the more structured versions of the interview found in survey methods. This is clearly demonstrated by Gold (1958) and Junker's (1960) work which described four theoretically possible roles which a sociologist, carrying out fieldwork, might adopt. Gold (1958) presents these roles as a continuum ranging from the complete participant to the complete observer; in between these extremes lie the participant-as-observer and the observer-as-participant. This last role, Gold says, is 'used in studies involving one-visit interviews'. If a label were to be placed on the research role which I took in this study, it would then be that of observer-as-participant.

The informal interview takes the superficial forms of a conversation. It is the underlying structure which distinguishes a purposeful interview from a social conversation. There is a fine balance between basing an interview on a series of research ideas and theoretical possibilities, while still allowing the respondent to introduce new thoughts and concepts. Considerable attention had to be given to the agenda, and the underlying sensitizing concepts which gave some theoretical direction to the interview. This style of interview contrasts sharply with that used in survey analysis. The structured interview seeks to achieve a standardization of data. But the lack of such standardization in the informal interview should not be seen as a threat to the validity of the data. Rather, it is a different means of using the technique in order to produce a full account of the phenomena under discussion. Cicourel's (1964: 108) rather acid comment upon the validity of *structured* interview data serves to underline the fact that what we are looking for in a research method is a match for the problem in hand. As he said: 'standardised questions with fixed choice answers provide a solution to the problem of meaning by simply avoiding it.'

If we take the survey analyst's criteria there will always be an inherent problem with the informal interview which seeks to obtain meaningful, valid, and reliable data. This problem stems from the necessary social interaction between interviewer and the interviewee. This is the very hallmark of the interpretive method. Indeed the interactionist's case turns on the very criticisms which survey methodologists level at the informal interview. The remarks of Bertrand Russell (1927: 30), quoted by Hyman (1954), in a discussion of the interview, might also serve as a humorous reminder of the difficulties we get into if we insist on judging research techniques according to inappropriate methodological and epistemological standpoints.

> 'The manner in which animals learn has been much studied in recent years, with a great deal of patient observation and experimentation. . . . One may say broadly that all the animals that have been carefully observed have behaved so as to confirm the philosophy in which the observer believed before the observation began. Nay more, they have all displayed the national characteristics of the observer. Animals studied by Americans rush about frantically, with an incredible display of hustle and pep, and at last achieve the desired result by chance. Animals observed by Germans sit still and think, and at last evolve the solution from their inner consciousness.'

Schatzman and Strauss (1973) discuss the way in which the interviewer must set a pattern where 'the interviewer does most of the leading and the respondent does most of the talking'. Thus the interviewer has an agenda, a selection of topics to be covered during the course of the interview, and must introduce these in such a way that it appears to the respondent that he is free to say whatever he wishes on the subject and, to some extent, dictate it. In other words, although the researcher has a clear aim in mind when using the informal interview, the method must be sufficiently flexible to accommodate new ideas during the course of the research. They describe such interviews usefully:

'The interviewer does not use a specific ordered list of questions or topics because this amount of formality would destroy the conversational style. He may have such a list in mind, or even in hand, but he is sufficiently flexible to order it in any way which seems natural to the respondent and to the interview situation. After all, what does one do when the respondent, while answering the first question, fully answers the third and sometimes questions six and seven? Far from being disorganised by this state of affairs, the interviewer builds upon what has apparently become a shared event. Conversation implies this very property.'

(Schatzman and Strauss 1973:73)

The researcher must have defined goals for the interview. Bogdan and Taylor (1975:108) say with reference to the interview: 'If you understand your goals, your subject and the interview situation, there is a wide latitude in what you can do. What is ultimately important is not your procedures but rather your frame of reference.' Although I had an agenda, the interviews with the students were conversational in style. This meant that the students introduced topics which they felt were relevant, rather than leaving it to me to dictate the content of the interview. The major appeal of this method is its flexibility. Rather than each informant being asked precisely the same questions, it allowed me to pursue topics which came up which had some conceptual promise, or indeed to introduce such ideas from earlier interviews to further develop a category. So I raised topics from my agenda, which included ward organization, talking with patients, and the socialization process. The data are treated as an accumulation of a body of information which is constantly being updated, elaborated, and refined, not as accumulated information to be analysed at a later stage.

Clearly, we can never know if informants are telling a story as they see it, or as they would have us believe they see it.

Nevertheless, certain steps can be taken to increase the chances of obtaining worthwhile data. In the case of the students two things seemed to be particularly important in this respect: first, that they should volunteer to be included in the study rather than be co-opted, and second, they should not see me to be in any way connected with their college or hospital 'establishment', and so feel able to trust me. My first problem in trying to create a 'non-establishment' image arose during my initial approach to the students. As this approach had to be made through the tutors, it tended to put the research on a formal footing. Although the tutors, as individuals, were very helpful, friendly, and interested in the research, when it came to introducing me to a group of students, they did so formally, calling me 'Miss Melia', even though I never introduce myself to anyone in that way. In doing this they conveyed to the students that the forthcoming session with me was compulsory, and so possibly undermined my chances of informality. This may be a trivial point, but as I had only twenty minutes or so in which to 'sell' the study and obtain volunteers, it was crucial that barriers should not be erected between the students and myself. To an extent I had anticipated this problem and always arrived in smart but casual clothes, trying not to appear to be anything which might be described as 'establishment' in the world of nursing. After the tutors left the room I reintroduced myself using my christian name, stressed that I was grateful for the students' time and, after a brief description of the study, invited anyone who was not interested, and might have other things to do, to feel free to leave. Throughout the research I emphasized whichever side of my dual role of research associate and postgraduate student at the university was most expedient at the time. I freely told the students that I was writing the study up for a doctoral thesis. This often created a feeling of comradeship, in the 'we are all students together' sense. It was also a useful means of creating the informal atmosphere which was desirable for the interview.

Once the initial approach had been made, the students showed a keen interest in the study and there was no difficulty in obtaining not only the volunteers who were eventually interviewed, but also another ten or so who were willing to be included in the study at a later stage if required. The interviews lasted on average from forty-five minutes to one hour. They mostly took place over coffee in the students' flats and were friendly, open, and conversational. The students were often quite relaxed about what they said, and some of the most revealing parts of the interviews followed remarks such as 'I shouldn't really say this, but . . .' or 'you won't tell them *I* said this, will you . . .'.

The last point to note about this research method is that all of the students interviewed were women. There were two or three men in each of the groups I approached, but I had asked for volunteers for whom this training was their first introduction to nursing. This served to rule out the two men who showed an interest in the study, as they were already qualified psychiatric nurses.

Analytic Procedures

In analysing these data I adopted the techniques of 'note' making as described by Schatzman and Strauss (1973). They discuss three types of 'notes' that the researcher might make: 'observational', 'theoretical', and 'methodological' notes. Their discussion relates to field research where the predominant method of data collection is participant observation, and thus 'observational notes' are defined as 'statements bearing upon events experienced principally through watching and listening. They contain as little interpretation as possible and are as reliable as the observer can construct them.' Each 'observational note' should stand by itself in so far as it can be understood in its own terms as an item of data. If the researcher wants to go further than the 'facts' he should, according to Schatzman and Strauss, write a 'theoretical note'. These notes 'represent self-conscious, controlled attempts to derive meaning from any one or several "observational notes".' In this way the researcher is able to make interpretations of an observation which has some conceptual future. A 'methodological note' relates to the research strategy rather than to the substantive area of study.

In my analysis, the 'observational notes' were the transcripts of the interviews and these consisted of verbatim sections of the interview. The 'theoretical' and 'methodological' notes were formulated as Schatzman and Strauss describe. The tapes were transcribed as soon as was possible after the interview. At that stage the main themes in the data were noted and preliminary theoretical notes made. When the data collection was complete, the transcripts were coded again and this time the theoretical notes were transfered onto index cards, along with the tape code so that the data could be recovered if necessary. New theoretical notes were also made at this stage as and when the further study of the transcripts dictated. At this point links between categories and potential categories also became apparent. During this process of analysis an original set of about thirty conceptual themes were combined and integrated by means of comparing items of data, making analytic searches and writing the interpretations of the data until the final categories were formulated.

REFERENCES

Abrahamson, M. (1967) *The Professional in the Organisation*. Rand McNally and Co.: Chicago.

Atkinson, P.A. (1983) The Reproduction of the Professional Community. In R. Dingwall and P. Lewis (eds) *The Sociology of the Professions: Lawyers, Doctors and Others*. Macmillan: London.

Baker, D.E. (1978) *Attitudes of Nurses to the Care of the Elderly*. Unpublished PhD thesis, University of Manchester.

Becker, H.S. (1962) The Nature of a Profession. In H.S. Becker (1970) *Sociological Work: Method and Substance*. Aldine: Chicago.

—— (1972) School is a Lousy Place to Learn Anything In. In B. Geer (ed.) (1972) *Learning to Work*. Sage: London.

—— and Geer, B. (1957) Participant Observation and Interviewing: A Comparison. *Human Organization* 16(3): 28–32.

——, ——, Hughes, E.C., and Strauss, A.L. (1961) *Boys in White*. University of Chicago Press: Chicago.

Bensman, J. and Gerver, I. (1963) Crime and Punishment in the Factory: The Function of Deviancy in Maintaining the Social System. *American Sociological Review* 38(4): 488–98.

Blau, P.M. and Scott, W.R. (1963) *Formal Organisations: A Comparative Approach*. Routledge and Kegan Paul: London.

Blumer, H. (1969) *Symbolic Interactionism: Perspective and Method*. Prentice Hall: Englewood Cliffs, NJ.

Bogdan, R. and Taylor, S.J. (1975) *Introduction to Qualitative Research Methods: A Phenomenological Approach to the Social Sciences*. John Wiley: New York.

Bosanquet, N. and Gerard, K. (1985) *Nursing Manpower: Recent Trends and Policy Options* Discussion paper 9. Centre for Health Economics: University of York.

Braverman, H. (1974) *Labor and Monopoly Capital. The Degredation of Work in the Twentieth Century*. Monthly Review Press: New York.

Bucher, R. and Strauss, A.L. (1961) Professions in Process. *American Journal of Sociology* 66: 325–34.

—— and Stelling, J.G. (1977) *Becoming Professional*. Sage: Beverly Hills.

Carpenter, M. (1977) The New Managerialism and Professionalism in Nursing. In M. Stacey, M. Reid, C. Heath, and R. Dingwall *Health and the Division of Labour*. Croom Helm: London.

Carr-Saunders, A.M. and Wilson, P.A. (1933) *The Professions*. The Clarendon Press: Oxford.

Cicourel, A.V. (1964) *Method and Measurement in Sociology*. Free Press: New York.

Clarke, M. (1978) Getting Through the Work. In R. Dingwall and J. McIntosh *Readings in the Sociology of Nursing*. Churchill Livingstone: Edinburgh.

Cressey, D.R. (1950) Criminal Violation of Financial Trust. *American Sociological Review* 15: 738–43.

Davies, C. (1976) Experience of Dependency and Control in Work: The Case of Nurses. *Journal of Advanced Nursing* 4: 273–82.

—— (1978) Four Events in Nursing History: A New Look. *Nursing Times* Occasional Papers 74(18): 69–71.

Davis, F. (1960) Uncertainty in Medical Prognosis, Clinical and Functional. *American Journal of Sociology* 66, 41–7.

Denzin, N.K. (1970) *The Research Act in Sociology. A Theoretical Introduction to Sociological Methods*. Butterworths: London.

Department of Health and Social Security (1972) Report of the Committee on Nursing (Cmnd. 5115 Chairman Briggs, A.). HMSO: London.

Dingwall, R. (1976) Accomplishing Profession. *Sociological Review* 24(2): 331–49.

—— (1977) *The Social Organisation of Health Visitor Training*. Croom Helm: London.

—— and McIntosh, J. (eds) (1978) *Readings in the Sociology of Nursing*. Churchill Livingstone: Edinburgh.

Ditton, J. (1977) Learning to 'Fiddle' the Customers – An Essay on the Organised Production of Part-time Theft. *Sociology of Work and Occupations* 4: 427–50.

Drucker, P.F. (1954) *The Practice of Management*. Harper and Row: New Occupations 4: 427–50.

Etzioni, A. (ed.) (1969) *The Semi-professions and their Organisation*. Free Press: New York.

Evans-Pritchard, E.E. (1940) *The Nuer*. Oxford University Press: Oxford.

Filstead, W.J. (ed.) (1970) *Qualitative Methodology: First-hand Involvement with the Social World*. Markham: Chicago.

Flexner, A. (1915) Is Social Work a Profession? In *Studies in Social Work* 4. New York School of Philanthropy.

Freidson, E. (1970a) *Profession of Medicine: A Study of the Sociology of Applied Knowledge*. Dodd, Mead & Co.: New York.

—— (1970b) *Professional Dominance: The Structure of Medical Care.* Aldine:Chicago.

Glaser, B.G. and Strauss, A.L. (1965) *Awareness of Dying.* Aldine: Chicago.

—— and —— (1967) *The Discovery of Grounded Theory: Strategies for Qualitative Research.* Aldine:Chicago.

Goffman, E. (1959) *The Presentation of Self in Everyday Life.* Doubleday and Co.:New York.

Gold, R.L. (1958) Roles in Sociological Field Observations. *Social Forces* 36:217–23.

Griffiths, E.R. (1983) *NHS Management Inquiry (letter to the Secretary of State).* London.

Hall, R.H. (1968) Professionalization and Bureaucratization. *American Sociological Review* 33:92–104.

Hardie, M. (1980) Auxiliaries in Nursing: Implications for the Division of Labour. Unpublished PhD thesis, University of Edinburgh.

—— and Hockey, L. (1978) *Nursing Auxiliaries in Health Care.* Croom Helm:London.

Henderson, V. (1966) *The Nature of Nursing.* Collier Macmillan:London.

Hughes, E.C. (1971) *The Sociological Eye.* Aldine:Chicago.

Hutt, R., Connor, H., and Hirsh, W. (1985) The Manpower Implications of Possible Changes in Basic Nurse Training. In Royal College of Nursing Commission *Annexe of Research Studies.* RCN:London.

Hyman, H.H. (1954) *Interviewing in Social Research.* University of Chicago Press:Chicago.

Inman, U. (1975) *Towards a Theory of Nursing Care.* Macmillan: London.

Johnson, M. (1978) Big Fleas Have Little Fleas – Nurse Professionalisation and Nursing Auxiliaries. In M. Hardie and L. Hockey (eds) (1978) *Nursing Auxiliaries in Health Care.* Croom Helm: London.

Johnson, T.J. (1972) *Professions and Power.* Macmillan:London.

Junker, B.H. (1960) *Fieldwork: An Introduction to the Social Sciences. Cases in Field Work.* University of Chicago Press:Chicago.

Lancet (1932) *Commission on Nursing.* Lancet:London.

Lupton, T. (1963) *On the Shop Floor.* Pergamon Press:Oxford.

McFarlane, J.K. (1976) A Charter for Caring. *Journal of Advanced Nursing* 1:187–96.

McIntosh, J. (1977) *Communication and Awareness in a Cancer Ward.* Croom Helm:London.

Mechanic, D. (1968) *Medical Sociology.* Free Press: New York.

Melia, K.M. (1981) *Student Nurses' Accounts of their Work and Training: A Qualitative Analysis.* Unpublished PhD thesis, University of Edinburgh.

Menzies, I. (1960) *A Case Study in the Function of Social Systems as a Defence Against Anxiety.* Tavistock:London.

Mercer, G.M., Kendall, P., and Reader, G. (eds) (1979) *The Employment of Nurses*. Croom Helm: London.

Merton, R.K., Reader, K., and Kendall, P.L. (eds) (1957) *The Student-Physician*. Harvard University Press: Cambridge, Mass.

Miller, S.J. (1970) *Prescription for Leadership: Training for the Medical Elite*. Aldine: Chicago.

Millerson, G. (1964) *The Qualifying Associations: A Study in Professionalization*. Routledge and Kegan Paul: London.

Ministry of Health, Scottish Home and Health Department (1966) Report of the Committee on Senior Nursing Staff Structure (Chairman Salmon, B.). HMSO: London.

Moult, A., Hockey, L., and Melia, K.M. (1978) *Patterns of Ward Organisation*. Unpublished report for Leverhulme Trustees. Nursing Studies Research Unit: University of Edinburgh.

Olesen, V. and Whittaker, E. (1968) *The Silent Dialogue: a Study of the Social Psychology of Professional Socialisation*. Jossey Bass: San Francisco.

Orem, D.E. (1971) *Nursing: Concepts of Practice*. McGraw Hill: New York.

Pape, R. (1964) Touristry: A Type of Occupational Mobility. *Social Problems* 11: 336–44.

Pill, R. (1970) The Sociological Aspects of the Case Study Sample. In M. Stacey, R. Dearden, R. Pill, and D. Robinson (1970) *Hospitals, Children and their Families*. Routledge and Kegan Paul: London.

Psathas, G. (1968) *The Student Nurse in the Diploma School of Nursing*. Springer: New York.

RCN (1943) *Report of the Nursing Reconstruction Committee* (Horder Report). RCN: London.

—— (1964) *A Reform of Nursing Education* (Platt Report). RCN: London.

Reid, N.G. (1985) *Wards in Chancery?* RCN: London.

Robinson, W.S. (1951) The Logical Structure of Analytic Induction. *American Sociological Review* 16: 812–18.

Rock, P. (1970) *The Making of Symbolic Interactionism*. Macmillan: London.

Roy, C. (1974) *Conceptual Models for Nursing Practice*. Appleton-Century-Crofts: New York.

Roy, D. (1952) Quota Restriction and Gold Bricking in a Machine Shop. *American Journal of Sociology* 57: 427–42.

—— (1954) Efficiency and the Fix. *American Journal of Sociology* 60: 255–66.

Russell, B. (1927) *Philosophy*. Norton: New York.

Schatzman, L. and Strauss, A.L. (1973) *Field Research: Strategies for a Natural Sociology*. Prentice Hall: Englewood Cliffs, NJ.

Schlotfeldt, R. (1975) The Need for a Conceptual Framework. In *Nursing Research I*. Little, Brown: Boston.

Scott, W.R. (1969) Professional Employees in a Bureaucratic Structure: Social Work. In A. Etzioni (1969) *The Semi-professions and their Organisation*. Free Press: New York.

Shortell, S.M. (1974) Occupational Prestige Differences within the Medical and Allied Health Professions. Social Science and Medicine 8: 1–9.

Stinchcombe, A.L. (1959) Bureaucratic and Craft Administration of Production: A Comparative Study. *Administrative Science Quarterly* 4: 168–87.

Strong, P.M. (1979) *The Ceremonial Order of the Clinic. Parents, Doctors and Medical Bureaucracies*. Routledge and Kegan Paul: London.

—— and Davis, A.G. (1977) Roles, Role Formats and Medical Encounters: A Cross-cultural Analysis of Staff–Client Relationships in Childrens' Clinics. *Sociological Review* 25 (4): 775–800.

Taylor, F.W. (1911) *The Principles of Scientific Management*. Harper Row: New York.

Trow, M. (1957) Comment on Participant Observation and Interviewing: A Comparison. *Human Organisation* 16(3): 33.

Volmer, H.W. and Mills, D.J. (eds) (1966) *Professionalisation*. Prentice Hall: Englewood Cliffs, NJ.

UKCC (1985) *Annual Report 1984–85*. United Kingdom Central Council for Nursing Midwifery and Health Visiting: London.

—— (1986) *Project 2000: A New Preparation for Practice*. United Kingdom Central Council for Nursing Midwifery and Health Visiting: London.

Weber, M. (1947) (trans. Henderson and Parsons) *The Theory of Social and Economic Organization*. William Hodge: London.

Williams, C.A. (1979) The Nature and Development of Conceptual Frameworks. In F.S. Downs and J.W. Fleming (1979) *Issues in Nursing Research*. Appleton-Century-Crofts: New York.

Znaniecki, F. (1934) *The Method of Sociology*. Farrer and Rinehart: New York.

INDEX